Mark Gardiner's

Ultimate Bathroom Book
of
Motorcycle Trivia

Copyright 2012, Bikewriter.com

Foreword

A note about the trials, tribulations, and trivialities of motorcycle journalism

A few years ago, I was approached by a small publisher to research and write a motorcycle trivia book. The advance they offered was embarrassingly small, but at the time, I had a few overdue credit card payments. I told the publisher, "Look, this is a terrible offer. Lucky for you guys, I'll take it. But you'd better come through with the advance in hurry."

The deal was, they were supposed to pay a portion of the advance up front, and the rest when the manuscript was delivered. The up-front payment never came, despite repeated (and increasingly strident) reminders from me. By the time I was ready to deliver the whole ms., I realized that while I was ready to hold up my end of the bargain, they were already 120 days late on the first payment. I strongly suspected that even if they made that payment, hell would have an NHL team before I ever saw the rest of the money.

So, I let the deadline lapse. The publisher, who had already listed the trivia book in their catalog for the following year, sent email after email asking for the text, to which I always gave the same response: Pay the advance, as per the contract, and I'll deliver the copy. This kind of foot-dragging by publishers drives authors crazy at the best of times, and it was happening right as the motorcycle enthusiast web sites were killing the print magazines that had been providing me with a meagre income.

While I waited for the publisher's advance, a few of my magazine clients coughed up some of the money they owed me, and thus emboldened, I finally gave the publisher an ultimatum: I told them they were in breach of contract, and had 48 hours to get me a check for the full amount of the advance, or I'd spike the job.

The check did come, in about 72 hours. But I was so mad that I scrawled "Contract Void" across it and mailed it back. I explained for the last time, to the idiot I'd been dealing with, that it had always been a crappy deal for me and that I'd only taken the job on because I needed the advance *when it had been promised*.

The publisher was outraged when I refused to turn over the manuscript, but the only thing I regretted was, I liked the book and wanted to see it published.

I don't know why it's taken me this long to print it myself, but at least this time around, I'm sure the publisher will pay me! It's been re-edited to 365 entries, so that you can put it by the john and flip it open once a day for a year. I hope you like it. If, however, you think it stinks, how can you be sure that odor isn't coming from right beneath you?

Motorcycling's first century – Ten decades defined

It's convenient for motorcycle historians that the history (so far) of the motorcycle coincides almost exactly with that of the Twentieth Century. The title "the first motorcycle" is usually awarded to a machine built by Gottlieb Daimler and William Maybach in 1885. But their contraption could also be described as the first car. It had two ungainly wooden wagon wheels fore and aft, with smaller stabilizing wheels off to the sides.

Hildebrand and Wolfmuller produced the first commercially viable motorcycle in 1894. This was also the first time the word "motorrad" (German for motorcycle) was used. Any modern motorcyclist would immediately recognize it as such: it had a gravity-feed fuel tank mounted above an internal-combustion motor; it rolled on air-filled rubber tires; the rider controlled it by means of a twistgrip and levers on a handlebar.

Power was transmitted to the rear wheel by steel rods, connected directly to the crankshaft. The rods were assisted on the return stroke by rubber bands! Despite its impressive displacement of 1488cc, Heinrich Hildebrand's motor only produced about 2.5 horsepower. It's not surprising that for the next twenty years or so, most motorcycles also had bicycle pedals, for assistance on hills or when extra oomph was required to pass a horse that was feeling his oats.

Day 1:

1900-'09: The de Dion-Bouton motor powers a revolution

Hundreds of small European workshops aspired to design and sell motorcycles. And why not? Anyone who could make a bicycle could make a motorcycle, if only they could find a small, reliable motor that made reasonable power and was available cheap.

Supplying those motors was the mission of two pioneering Frenchmen, Count Albert de Dion, and Georges Bouton. They patented a small, high-speed gas engine that they used in automobiles of their own design. What is more important, they also sold thousands of motors and licensed their design to over 150 motorcycle companies.

Day 2:

1910-'19: Alfred Angus Scott shows that a motorcycle can be more than a bicycle with an auxiliary motor

Scott was the holder of more than sixty patents. His eponymous motorcycles were among the first to feature kick-starters, chain drives, and multi-speed gearboxes. He usually used simple two-stroke motors that were water-cooled – about 60 years before such cooling was "pioneered" by Suzuki and introduced with great fanfare on the GT 750.

Day 3:

1920-'29: The motorcycle goes upmarket

The roar in "Roaring Twenties" was the sound of an overheated stock market, not motorcycles. However, it was a great decade for hundreds of now-vanished manufacturers.

George Brough was a motorcycle maker who really captured the spirit of the times. His Brough Superior models were "the Rolls-Royce of motorcycles" and that wasn't an empty boast – the bikes were so well made that when Charles Rolls and William Royce examined one of them, they gave Brough permission to use their names in his advertising.

Most Brough Superiors were sold with engines outsourced from James A. Prestwich. Those "JAP" motors were supplied to many other builders, but Brough's came in special tunings that allowed him to guarantee that his SS100 model would really go 100 miles an hour. Each of Brough's machines was specially fitted to its owner, like a custom suit. They were fast, comfortable and built to last, so it's not surprising they remain sought after to this day.

Day 4:

1930-'39: Motorcycles cure depression, but not *the* Depression

Excelsior (which made fine big V-twins) and Henderson (known for smooth inline fours) both went bust in '31.

Indian had been acquired by the wealthy E. Paul duPont but even his resources couldn't prevent a precipitous drop in sales. The company had sold

40,000 machines to the Army alone in WWI, but shipped just 1,660 motorcycles in 1933. Indeed, Indian never really regained sound health.

Harley-Davidson managed to get through the depression on the strength of strong fleet sales. The Motor Company dominated the market for police motorcycles and introduced the 3-wheeled "Servicar" delivery vehicle in 1932. Harley even sold fan-cooled versions of its big V-twin engines for use as industrial powerplants.

One bright spot in this otherwise, well, depressing period was the adoption of The Motorcyclist as the official magazine of the American Motorcyclist Association. The magazine, which was already well established, still exists today. Among motorcycle magazines, only the German monthly "Das Motorrad" has been published longer.

Day 5:

1940-'49: You're in the Army now

America's belated entry into WWII kick-started Indian again and breathed new life into Harley, too. Both companies filled open-ended military procurement contracts for all the bikes they could make, at the standard cost-plus-10% rate. Harley alone sold over 90,000 45 cu. in. WL models.

Day 6:

1950-'59: "What are you rebelling against?" "What have you got?"

After the war, G.I.s came home with ready cash, an appreciation for the motorcycles they'd seen "over there" and – shall we say – a heightened sense of what constituted excitement. In 1947 this led to the so-called "Hollister motorcycle riot". That event received national prominence when a beefy drunk, slumped on his motorcycle, was pictured in Life magazine.

In 1954, the reputation of motorcyclists was sealed by The Wild One, a film based on Hollister and starring Marlon Brando as a disaffected rebel.

Ironically, in the late '40s the Hells Angels were still an AMA-sanctioned club that organized races and rallies. But by the time the '50s drew to a close the 'Angels were outlaws who made Brando's "Johnny" seem like a schoolboy. It's not clear if art imitated life, or if life imitated art.

Day 7:

1960-'69: "You meet the nicest people on a Honda"

In '62, American Honda sold 40,000 motorcycles through its 750-dealer network. When management set a target of 200,000 units the following year, Honda's ad agency, Grey, knew they had their work cut out for them.

Grey's creative types proposed a set of print ads showing students, women and couples – not the "typical" motorcyclists – on Honda's 50cc step-through Cub. The ads proclaimed, "You meet the nicest people on a Honda". In 1964 Grey produced a "nicest people" TV ad that ran during the Academy Awards.

The campaign not only launched Honda in the U.S. market, it redeemed the image of motorcycling as a whole.

Day 8:

1970-'79: The "Japanese Invasion" gets reinforcements

Throughout this decade Yamaha, Suzuki, and Kawasaki all established themselves as serious rivals to Honda – to the chagrin of Harley-Davidson (which lobbied hard for protective tariffs) and to the ultimate demise of the entire British motorcycle industry.

The iconic '70s muscle bike was the Kawasaki Z1. The company had a 750cc four-cylinder bike in development when Honda unveiled the CB750 in '68. So they went back to the drawing board and created the 903cc Z1. It reached the market five years later. The dual-overhead cam motor made an honest 80+ hp and propelled the bike to 130mph.

Day 9:

1980-'89: "Can't come in to work today boss, gotta' ride my 'Gixxer'!"

The modern superbike originated with the 100-horsepower Suzuki GSX-R750 in 1985. How stunning was it? Kevin Cameron, Cycle's savvy reviewer (who had seen the state of the art when he'd been a Grand Prix mechanic) was moved to wonder, "Where do motorcycles go from here?"

The "Gixxer" put genuine racetrack performance under anyone with $4,500 to spend. It weighed just 388 pounds – two pounds less than the *minimum* weight specified in the rules for the AMA's Superbike class. It was as addictive as cocaine and, in the wrong hands, about as destructive a habit.

Day 10:
1990-'99: The beginning of a motorcycle Renaissance

Motorcycle sales peaked in the early '70s when the baby boomers were reckless teens and twentysomethings. The late '70s and '80s saw a long decline that finally reversed itself when the 'boomers hit their mid-life crises. With a flood of money pouring into both domestic and import dealerships, there was a demand for bigger and more comfortable cruisers as well as faster and more exotic sport bikes.

Harley-Davidson sales *increased 400%* between '90 and '99. The resurgent market came too late for Italy's Cagiva company, which found itself in a cash crunch. The private investment firm Texas Pacific Group took a controlling interest in Cagiva's famous Ducati line and turned it into one of the world's most recognized luxury brands. TPG saved a great company, allowing it to give us some of the most beautiful bikes ever made. Then they took it public at huge profit. Maybe Gordon Gecko was right when he said, "Greed is good."

Engineering advances that led to the modern motorcycle

Modern motorcycles pack so much technology and so much performance into small – and surprisingly affordable – packages that we should all be careful not to let the government realize how much fun we're having, or they'll find a way to tax our riding pleasure!

Seriously though, getting to where we are today took a series of engineering advances that almost all first appeared a surprisingly long time ago. Many of the gizmos on modern bikes were developed for use in aircraft, another field in which powerful, lightweight motors were highly valued. Others were invented and perfected by creative engineers in several locations at about the same time, or were invented long before they could be made commercially viable.

Here are ten key stages in the evolution of one very intelligent design: the modern sport bike.

Day 11:
The "Rover" bicycle
The first motorcycles were all essentially bicycles to which a small auxiliary motor was fitted. Thus, for motorcycles to become practical, bicycles first had to become safe to ride. That was definitely not the case when the only bicycles were "penny farthings" with enormous front wheels – they were hard to get on and pedal and even worse, when riders fell, they crashed to the ground from seats as much as six feet high.

In the 1880s, the first bicycles with two small wheels, a low seat, and chain drive appeared. This basic design came to be known as the "safety frame" and was patented by the Rover bicycle company.

Day 12:
Pneumatic tires
Early bicycles were called "bone shakers" because they ran on steel-shod wooden wheels. Considering that most roads of the period were paved with cobblestones, the name was an understatement. At about the same time as the safety frame bicycle made riding safe, an Irish veterinarian named Dunlop invented the air-filled rubber tire, making bicycles reasonably comfortable.

Day 13:
Throttle control
Here's a note from the Department of Scary Thoughts: many early motorcycle "carburetors" were just pans of gasoline that were heated by an open flame. Vapors produced that way were then burned in the cylinders. Back then, "crash and burn" was not

simply a figure of speech.

Spray carburetors were obviously much safer, but early carbs lacked throttles. Riders controlled speed by simply choking the air intake, or by changing their spark advance.

Oscar Hedstrom, the engineer behind Indian "motocycles" was one of the first people to devise a throttle-controlled carburetor. That was in 1901.

Day 14:
Overhead valves, four-valve heads
Hedstrom wasn't finished incorporating some very creative innovations into Indians. Board track racing was very popular and an important way for Indian to promote sales. In order to make a more powerful motor, Hedstrom knew he needed to incorporate overhead valves. The problem was they were more prone to breakage, causing catastrophic engine damage. As early as 1911 he solved this problem by using four valves per cylinder instead of two (thus making each valve lighter and easier to open and close). The result was a motor capable of propelling the flimsy board track racers of the day, which were unencumbered by brakes of any kind, to nearly 120 miles an hour!

Day 15:
Water cooling
The very first internal-combustion motorcycle, built by Daimler and Maybach in the 1880s, was water cooled, but it also had four wheels. The first two-wheeled motorcycle with a water-cooled motor may have been the 850cc Wilkinson TMC built around

1910. It leaned to turn, but had a steering wheel and a chair instead of a saddle, so it was also perhaps too car-like to truly be called a motorcycle.

In 1914, the Scott TS set a surprising precedent. It had a 486cc two-stroke, twin-cylinder motor that bore an amazing resemblance to sport bikes like the Yamaha RZ350, produced a full seventy years later.

Day 16:
Disc brakes
This was a rare area of technology where cars were ahead of bikes, partly because cars' heavier weight made braking more of a challenge and because it was easier for automotive engineers to incorporate early hydraulic systems, which were quite bulky. The idea of disc brakes dated way back to 1901, when Frederick William Lanchester patented a brake that operated on a car's clutch plate.

In the early '60s, the tiny Mini Cooper rally car had disc brakes and these units attracted the attention of motorcycle racers. Canadian Grand Prix racing star Mike Duff was one of the first racers to adapt Mini Cooper brakes to his Yamaha 250.

Day 17:
Electronic ignition
At least one inventor, in Denmark, managed to prototype a working CDI (capacitor discharge ignition) in 1965. His prototype was installed on a 90cc Kawasaki, which might have been his problem: those bikes already had reliable ignitions with conventional points. A few years later, however, a

large English bike shop – Boyer of Bromley – finally got tired of the notoriously unreliable Lucas ignitions their racing team's Triumph Bonnevilles. They contracted Ernie Bransden to design an electronic ignition. Their Boyer-Bransden electronic ignitions are still sold to people wanting to make old bikes start and run more reliably.

Day 18:
Monoshock
The fabulous Vincent Black Shadow featured a prescient rear swingarm and shock design, but it came and went. The modern single-shock rear end however, came to sport bikes from motocross. It traces its lineage back to the 1975 Yamaha YZ motocrossers. Those bikes were updated in '77 and carried Bob Hannah to the first of many AMA motocross and supercross titles.

Day 19:
Aluminum Beam Frame
Most modern motorcycles feature a beam frame that connects the steering head to the swingarm pivot in a nearly straight line. This stiff, light design sprang from the imagination of an influential Spanish engineer named Antonio Cobas. In 1983 his JJ Kobas 250cc Grand Prix racer was the first bike with such a frame. It was quickly copied by other Grand Prix racing teams and then into streetbike frames, such as the first Yamaha "Deltabox" chassis which first appeared on the manic TZR250 repli-racer in 1985.

Day 20:
Fuel injection
Once again, motorcycles were "behind" cars in terms of adopting this particular technology. Initial attempts to make fuel injectors work on motorcycles were held back by size and weight concerns and by the fact that high performance motorcycle handling is influenced by the rider's ability to open the throttle and feed in power very smoothly. The first production motorcycle fitted with electronic fuel injection was the 1982 Honda CX500 Turbo. That model was a technological triumph but a commercial failure. As is often the case however, both the CX500 Turbo and its big brother CX650 are now highly collectible.

Most influential engineers and designers

Before the modern motorcycle could take shape, it first took shape in the minds of engineers and designers. Picking the double handful most deserving of this list is a task guaranteed to infuriate some readers, but these ten were all geniuses and each left his mark on motorcycling for decades.

Day 21:
Pietro Remor – established basic design of modern superbikes

In the late 1930s, Remor created a revolutionary Italian racing motorcycle called the Rondine. It featured four cylinders, water cooling and supercharging. After WWII, supercharging was banned in Grand Prix racing. Remor took his motor to the Gilera company and recast it as an upright, air-cooled, dual-overhead cam four.

Remor's design established the across-the-frame four-cylinder motor as the layout for most of the high-performance motorcycles made since 1950. When Gilera withdrew from racing, Remor took his skills and patterns to MV Agusta. Motors he designed won world championships for three different companies in five different decades.

Day 22:

Walter Kaaden – doubled the horsepower of two-stroke motors

As the head of engineering and racing at MZ in communist-controlled East Germany, Kaaden faced challenges that dwarfed those of engineers on the other side of the iron curtain – materials shortages, travel restrictions, and a dispirited workforce, to name just a few. Despite those handicaps, in the late 1950s and early '60s, he made some of the world's fastest motorcycles. His secret was the expansion-chamber exhaust, which doubled the power output of two-stroke motors.

For years, he alone understood the arcane physics math of expansion-chamber design. Then one of his riders, Ernst Degner escaped to the West, bringing the knowledge with him. The next year, Degner rode a Suzuki (bearing a conspicuous resemblance to an MZ) to a world title. Virtually every two-stroke motor built since then used an exhaust based on Kaaden's research.

Day 23:

Yoshiro Harada – led development of the Honda CB750

It is impossible to overstate the impact of the first truly mass-production four-cylinder, disc-braked motorcycle. When the CB750 was unveiled at the 1968 Tokyo Motor Show consumers gasped and the world press (and rival companies) were taken by surprise. It had been developed by a small team working in total secrecy. The team leader was Yoshiro Harada.

Harada toured the United States a few years earlier, meeting American riders and Honda motorcycle dealers when Honda introduced the CB450 twin. That bike had sold poorly in America despite the fact that it outperformed much bigger British twins. He realized that the U.S. with its wide-open spaces, would embrace a big, powerful bike. The decision to make it 750cc was based on the knowledge that Triumph and BSA were developing 750cc triples. It would be a four-cylinder bike to evoke Honda's Grand Prix racing heritage (and one-up the English). Finally, it would produce at least 67 horsepower, since the most powerful Harleys made 66!

The design was a breakthrough, but so was the design *process*. Harada's team was able to prototype the bike in record time and ensure an efficient manufacturing process by making revolutionary use of computer-assisted-design and computer-assisted-manufacturing. The end result established Honda once and for all as the world's preeminent motorcycle manufacturer.

Day 24:
Edward Turner – father of British twins
Turner was born on the day King Edward was crowned, which was appropriate as Turner himself became British motorcycle "royalty." When he was hired as Triumph's General Manager and Chief Designer he was offered a lavish salary and 5% of the company stock and profits!

Soon after, he designed the 1937 Speed Twin. In truth, the motor was not strikingly innovative –

some say Turner just copied its basic architecture from the Riley 9 car in which he was chauffeured to work. However, it made elegant use of existing technology and established the basic design for all British twins between the end of WWII and the 1970s. For much of that time, bikes like the Triumph Bonneville were the most sought-after models in the market.

Day 25:
Phil Vincent – created the innovative and powerful Black Shadow
Between the late 1920s and mid-'50s, Vincent's motorcycles were among the fastest and most advanced on the market. He was the first major manufacturer to use a single rear shock absorber but the most striking aspect of his design was the way he virtually did away with the frame altogether. After WWII when high-quality steel was in short supply in Britain, he attached the steering head to the front of his massive V-twin motor and pivoted the swingarm from the back of it. Today's manufacturers are still catching up to Vincent's ideas.

Day 26:
Fabio Taglione – adapted Daimler's desmodromic valve concept to motorcycles
Taglione was the chief designer at Ducati from 1954-'89. Although many "Ducatisti" would like to believe that Ducati invented the "desmo" valve system (using a second cam to close the valves, instead of valve springs) the patent was held by Daimler-Benz. Still, it was Taglione who realized that

the system would benefit fast-revving motorcycle engines which, in the 1950s, were limited by the reliability of valve springs. When he mated two Ducati 350cc singles to create the first Ducati 90-degree V-twin, he created one of motorcycling's truly iconic designs.

Day 27:
Etsuo Yokouchi – Suzuki GSX-R750 design team leader
Every contemporary Japanese "race replica" motorcycle owes a debt to the first Suzuki GSX-R750, which was launched at the 1984 Cologne motorcycle show. The rest of the world got the new bike in '85, while American riders chomped at the bit for another year. It was so light, powerful and advanced for its day that Cycle World's supremely experienced Kevin Cameron mused, "Where will motorcycles go from here?"

Day 28:
Tadao Baba – creator of the Honda Fireblade
Thanks to the GSX-R750, Suzuki stole a march on Honda in the performance market. Then Suzuki introduced a larger and even faster 1100cc "gixxer." That bike, however, didn't handle nearly so well. Baba, an engineer working at Honda saw the opportunity to create a motorcycle with open-class power and 750-class handling. When it was introduced in 1992, the 'blade amply reached those goals: it weighed about 410 pounds and produced nearly 125 horsepower. Baba's creation completely changed the expectations of open class riders, who

had always wanted acceleration and top speed but never knew they could have handling too.

Day 29:
William S. Harley – Harley-Davidsons are all V-twins because of him
Bill Harley drew up a single-cylinder motor suitable for powering a bicycle in 1901, at the age of 21. Two years later he partnered with Arthur Davidson to produce a racing motorcycle; that first Harley-Davidson was born in a 150 square-foot shed. Harley graduated from the University of Wisconsin with a degree in mechanical engineering in 1907. By that time, two more Davidson brothers had joined the partnership and the company was firmly established. Harley designed and prototyped the first H-D V-twin motor that year, too.

Day 30:
Erik Buell – engineering iconoclast
Although Harley-Davidson's air-cooled, pushrod V-twin motors are not an obvious choice as powerplants, Erik Buell's determination to produce a mass-market American sport bike is admirable and he's proven to be an extremely creative engineer. His use of shock absorber springs that operate in tension, frames that carry fuel and swingarms that carry oil, and rim-mounted brake discs are just a few of the inventions that may, someday, be found on all high-performance motorcycles.

Entrepreneurs that made things happen

It's hard to make a good motorcycle. Maybe it's even harder to make money making motorcycles – but if it wasn't possible to do so, we'd have nothing to ride! Here are the most influential motorcycle entrepreneurs.

Day 31:
Soichiro Honda – an individualist in a nation that prized conformists

The son of a village blacksmith, Honda was exposed to bicycles when they were brought into his father's shop for repair. He had only a primary school education, but showed a striking aptitude for both engineering and business. Before starting the Honda Motor Company to make motorized bicycles in postwar Japan, he had already built up two successful businesses, one supplying piston rings to Toyota, and another making propellers for the Japanese air force.

Mr. Honda was anything but a typical Japanese businessman. A rugged individualist, he refused to participate in the "keiretsu" alliances between companies, which typically gave big banks a strong influence in business decisions. When virtually all Japanese motorbikes had noisy, smelly two-stroke motors he decided to make a four-stroke. That typified a willingness to plan and invest for long-term success even if it meant ignoring prevailing "wisdom." One of the motorcycles that benefited from that insight was the Super Cub step-through. It was introduced in 1958 and is still produced almost unmodified today. Honda recently sold the 50 millionth Super Cub, making it the best selling vehicle of all time.

Day 32:
George Hendee – two wheel demon, and dreamer
Hendee was one of the most successful bicycle racers in Massachusetts at the turn of the century – at one point, he won 302 races out of 309! He started a company making his own bicycles, which sold well, thanks to his racing reputation.

Many of the very first motorcycles were "pacers" used to train bicycle racers. They were typically unreliable but Hendee noticed that Oscar Hedstrom's ran very well. In 1901, Hendee approached Hedstrom and told him that his dream was to start a company devoted to making motorized bicycles. They called their company Indian, and in short order it was America's leading motorcycle manufacturer. In 1912, Indian sold over 20,000 units.

Day 33:
Arthur Davidson – built H-D dealer network
While his friend Bill Harley and to a lesser extent the other Davidson brothers provided the technical know-how, the early business success of Harley-Davidson was largely due to Arthur Davidson. In 1910 he set out to enroll a national network of dealers. He also recognized the importance of factory-training for dealer service staff, and the importance of advertising if H-D was ever to surpass Indian in annual sales.

Day 34:

Vaughn Beals – saved the Harley-Davidson brand

By the mid-'70s after years of AMF mismanagement, Harley-Davidson had lost almost all customer loyalty and profits were in freefall. When a group of company executives led by Vaughn Beals offered to buy the division for $75 million, AMF quickly agreed.

After the 1981 leveraged buyout, Beals led an amazing corporate turnaround. He funded new product development and implemented world-class quality control. It's impossible to know what would have happened to the H-D brand if Beals had not risen up to save it, but it's certain that no one else could have done a better job at rehabilitating it.

Day 35:

John Bloor – rebooted Triumph

Like Harley-Davidson, Triumph was a company that had fallen on hard times – more than once. In the 1920s the company made an ill-fated move to produce cars as well and in 1936 an entrepreneur named Jack Sangster drove a hard bargain, acquiring the motorcycle business at a good price. Sangster's business instincts nearly make him worthy of a place on this list, too. He hired the brilliant Edward Turner and after turning a handsome profit on sales, sold the company to BSA for another big payday in 1951.

From the mid-'70s through the mid-'80s Triumph died an agonizingly slow death. The brand almost vanished altogether. Luckily John Bloor, a real estate developer, bought the old factory in Meriden. Against all advice, Bloor decided to build a new factory in nearby Hinckley. He spent millions designing new motorcycles that were unveiled at the Cologne Motorcycle Show in 1990. While those first "new" Triumphs got mixed reviews, the company has shown a remarkable willingness to go its own way, producing a line of unique machines that again have earned it a devoted fan base.

Day 36:
Count Domenico Agusta – kept racing in Italian blood
This Italian Count ran MV Agusta during its heyday between the end of WWII and the early '70s. During that time, the company was really a helicopter manufacturer with a small motorcycle subsidiary. The road-going motorcycles they made would never warrant including the Count on this list, but thanks to his own fierce pride and competitive streak, the company also funded the greatest Grand Prix racing team of all time.

When the Japanese factories began to dominate in the late '60s, they drove out most of the Italian marques. By lavishing funds from the helicopter business on his racing team, Agusta single-handedly preserved Italian racing honor.

Day 37:
Malcolm Forbes – nothing and everything to do with motorcycles
Forbes was the son of America's first business magazine publisher. After heroic service in WWII, he came home to work at Forbes Magazine, although he nearly became the Governor of New Jersey – he won

the Republican nomination but lost the election. So what does running Forbes Magazine have to do with motorcycles? Nothing.

Forbes discovered motorcycling in the 1960s. He bought a motorcycle dealership in New Jersey, which became one of the biggest shops in the country. Using his high-level business connections, he worked tirelessly to establish motorcycle riding as a respectable pastime. He was an extremely effective political lobbyist always ready to defend motorcycling from legal assault. With his media-savvy background, he managed to plant scores of motorcycle stories in the mainstream media. The social acceptability of motorcycles today owes much to Malcolm Forbes, even though in his heyday, he was a closeted gay man who spent his nights in gay 'bath-houses' that most mainstream Americans would have found utterly shocking.

Day 38:
Floyd Clymer – serial entrepreneur
Clymer was already famous as a young teenager – at 13 (in 1909) he was the youngest Ford dealer in the country! He went on to become a winning motorcycle racer and soon had a dealership for Harley-Davidson and Excelsior motorcycles in his home state of Colorado. He was an innovative marketer and one of the first people to sell motorcycles to police departments and delivery businesses. In his early 20s he began publishing his first motorcycle magazine.

His career was put on hold when he served a year in federal prison for mail fraud. He had been offered a chance to plead guilty and avoid prison altogether but he always claimed he was innocent and refused to admit a crime he didn't commit. When he got out of prison he took over the distribution of Indian motorcycles on the West coast. Here again, he had marketing savvy, arranging for Indian motorcycles to appear in films and lending them to Hollywood stars. When Indian faltered in the '50s, Clymer desperately tried to save the brand but failed. He also was briefly the importer of the eyebrow-raising Munch Mammoth motorcycle.

Last but not least, he was the publisher of Cycle Magazine from the early '50s to the mid-'60s and ran a very successful business publishing motorcycle repair manuals.

Day 39:
George Barber – collector, track builder, philanthropist once known as 'The Ice Cream Man from Hell'

Barber was a sports car racer who gave up the track to take over the family business, Barber Dairies, based in Birmingham Alabama. He built it into the largest privately-owned dairy in the Southeast and then, late in life, assembled the world's most important collection of vintage motorcycles.

When the collection outgrew its original home in one of the old dairy warehouses, he built Barber Motorsports Park. The park includes one of the best race-tracks in the U.S., and the best motorcycle museum in the world. After spending $60 million of his own money, Barber gave the park to the city of Birmingham and the state of Alabama.

Day 40:

"Big" Bill France – promoted the Daytona 200

France is best known as the father of NASCAR the builder of Daytona International Speedway, France was also a motorcycle racer. The city of Daytona Beach persuaded the AMA to hold the 200-mile national championship race there in 1937. After a few lackluster years, it seemed Daytona would lose the race, until France was persuaded to become the promoter. He continued to promote the race but realized that it could not continue on the beach. He opened his track in 1959 and the AMA saw the light and moved the race there two years later. Under France's control, the race became an international sensation.

Sisters have *always* been doin' it for themselves

In recent years, the Motorcycle Safety Foundation has reported that a third to half of the students in most new rider training classes are women. And Elena Myers recently made history by becoming the first woman ever to win an AMA Pro Racing road race. But one thing's for sure – not all women are newcomers. History shows that there have always been avid, expert female motorcyclists.

Day 41:
Linda Dugeau – The original "Motor Maid"
In the '30s, there was an association of female aviators called the "Ninety-nine Club". This inspired Linda to form a similar association of female motorcyclists. She teamed up with Dot Robinson, a well-known competition rider, to form a club called the "Motor Maids".

It took Linda and Dot several years to find the 50 members they needed to earn an AMA charter, but the Motor Maids were soon known for their smart uniforms, complete with white gloves. The club still exists, with branches across the U.S. and in Eastern Canada. (www.motormaids.org)

Day 42:
Dot Robinson – Sidecar champion
Dot's father, James Goulding, was the designer of a popular line of motorcycle sidecars. When Dot's mother went into labor with her, Goulding took her to the hospital in a sidecar. As an adult, Dot and her husband were Harley-Davidson dealers in Detroit.

When she won a Jack Pine enduro in the sidecar class, she became the first woman ever to win an AMA national competition. She rode until she was well into her 80s, often in a pink riding suit that she adopted in the 1950s, when the customary black leather outfits became associated with outlaw gangs.

Day 43:
Linda Wallach and Florence Blenkiron – Taking the Rugged Road
Linda grew up in the 1930s, in the English midlands near the factories where BSAs and Triumphs were manufactured. Despite her early fascination with bikes and her obvious skill as a rider, she was never encouraged to pursue such an unladylike sport.

Undeterred, she studied engineering and later took her friend Florence on an epic sidecar journey across the Sahara and south all the way to Cape Town, South Africa. The women had to argue their way past French Foreign Legion outposts and face man-eating lions (luckily they weren't woman-eaters). They rebuilt their engine in mid-journey and once pushed their rig 25 miles. They told the whole story in a popular book titled, "The Rugged Road."

Linda later became the first woman to earn a coveted "Gold Star" for lapping the Brooklands race oval at over 100 miles an hour. In WWII she became the first woman ever to serve as a British military dispatch rider.

After the war, she moved to the U.S. where she worked as a motorcycle mechanic, eventually owning her own dealership. She wrote a popular motorcycle training manual, then moved to Phoenix where she operated a riding school. She helped found WIMA, the Women's International Motorcycle Association. She never owned a car and rode until her eyesight failed at the age of 88. She died less than two years after giving up her beloved sport.

Day 44:
Bessie Stringfield – The Motorcycle Queen of Miami

The American Motorcycle Association's "Bessie Stringfield Award" is given to women who distinguish themselves in the sport of motorcycling.

As an African-American woman in the '30s and '40s, Bessie made several well-publicized cross-country rides, fearlessly taking on both racists and sexists. She was frequently denied accommodation and there are pictures of her sleeping right on her motorcycle. Once, she was run off the road. Those experiences didn't dim her patriotism however – during WWII she served as the U.S. military's first female dispatch rider.

Bessie was truly a larger-than-life character. She once disguised herself as a man to win a dirt track race. She said she'd owned 27 Harley-Davidsons and one Indian. She owned up to no less than six husbands, too.

Day 45:
Margaret Wilson – "Most Popular and Typical"
Margaret was a partner, with her husband, in Wilson's Motorcycle Sales in Cedar Rapids, Iowa. She helped organize the Corn State Riders Motorcycle Club and was the only woman member of the club's precision drill team. Not all of her riding was in parades, however – one year, she rode through all 48 contiguous states. In 1958, she was awarded a large trophy from the AMA, proclaiming her to be "The Most Popular and Typical Girl Rider".

Day 46:
Marjorie Cottle – Rode in motorcycling's real "Great Escape"
Marjorie Cottle was one of the first female competitors in the International Six Day Trial, which is often called "the Olympics of motorcycling."

In 1939, the ISDT was held in Nazi-controlled Austria in the last few days before England declared war on Germany. That year, Britain sent both a civilian and a military team to compete. After four days, when it seemed that war could break out at any minute, British officials told the civilian team to return to England immediately. Cottle refused to leave and competed on the fifth day alongside the British Army team. When they too were ordered to abandon competition, Cottle and the Army team rode their motorcycles to neutral territory in Switzerland.

Day 47:
Debbie Evans – Trials, not tribulations
Debbie was born in Southern California in the late
'50s. "I think they wanted a boy," she said about of
her parents. Debbie grew up competing in trials and
enduros, long before there were separate classes for
girls. Not that she needed them – she was soon
beating all the boys. She was the first woman to
compete in a round of the trials World Championship,
and finished fourth in the 175cc class of the grueling
Scottish Six Day Trial. After retiring from
competition she became one of Hollywood's leading
stuntwomen.

Day 48:
Angelle Sampey – Life's a drag
Angelle was the NHRA Pro Stock Bike drag racing
champion in 2000. She proved that season was no
fluke by winning the title again the next two years,
making her the most successful female motorcycle
racer in U.S. history.

Being five-foot nothing and weighing
barely100 pounds doesn't prevent Angelle from
manhandling a 320 horsepower Suzuki that covers
1/4 mile in about 7 seconds. Maybe her ability to
wrestle that beast is enhanced by her other passion –
the no-holds-barred martial art of Brazilian ju-jitsu.

Day 49:

Katja Poensgen – Don't hate her because she's beautiful

Katja, born in 1976, was the daughter of a German motocross racer and loved everything to do with speed. After working her way up through the German supersport ranks, she became the first woman Grand Prix racer in the modern era.

In truth, her GP results were meager. Her detractors said she was there on the strength of her looks and not talent, but she was never given the best of equipment – in a bigger and better-funded team she might have been more competitive. One thing is certain: in the 2001 Italian GP at Mugello, she rode smoothly and well in torrential rain. By finishing 14th, she became the first woman ever to score points in a modern Grand Prix.

"Nice bike! What is it?" Top stylists and customizers

Whether they're professional stylists working for big motorcycle manufacturers, or customizers working on one bike at a time in small workshops, here are the guys whose work draws crowds.

Day 50:
Massimo Tamburini
Tamburini was the "ta" in the great-but-under-funded Bimota company. Although he designed a number of beautiful bikes for Bimota, the company is best remembered for the futuristic "Tesi." After leaving Bimota he moved to Ducati where he created the iconic Ducati 916. Later still, he penned the MV Agusta F4, which tops the list of the world's most beautiful motorcycles. 'Nuff said.

Day 51:
William G. Davidson
Known to the Harley faithful simply as "Willie G.," he is the grandson of H-D founder William A. Davidson. Willie G. studied graphic art at the University of Wisconsin and then attended the prestigious Pasadena Art Center College of Design. He was in California at a time when the motorcycle custom scene was booming and brought a much more radical styling sensibility back to Wisconsin when he went to work in the family business.

The old guard at The Motor Company may have resented his newfangled designs, but the FX Super Glide and the XLCR definitely attracted attention at a time when the company needed all the help (and any good publicity) it could get. He was one of the executives who, under Vaughn Beals, bought the company back from AMF, and became VP of Design, and the company's ambassador.

Day 52:
Craig Vetter
Until he came along, only racing motorcycles had fairings. Vetter studied design at the University of Illinois in the 1960s and rode a Yamaha 305. On his first long highway ride, he realized that fighting the constant wind-blast was exhausting. When he settled in close behind a semitrailer and the buffeting stopped, a light bulb went off above his head. He went home and carved his first fairing shape out of Styrofoam, then got a local boat builder to give him a crash course in fiberglass lay-up.

In the early '70s, the flood of powerful new motorcycles like the Honda 750 provided a ready market for Vetter's Windjammer fairings. He was also asked to style an American-market version of the BSA Rocket III. BSA went bust before it could go into production but it saw the light of day soon after as the Triumph Hurricane. He sold his Vetter fairings business in '78 but continued to do some very interesting custom work. In 1980, he built the "Mystery Ship," based on a Kawasaki KZ1000.

Although it was far ahead of its time, it was priced out of the market: when a stock KZ sold for $3,500, Vetter's creation went for a cool ten grand.

Day 53:
Anonymous "Bobber" builders
After WWII, hundreds of thousands of young American men were demobilized. They returned to the U.S. with time on their hands and money in their pockets. Next, they did what men in such positions have always done: bought motorcycles.

In the late '40s and early '50s, it became fashionable to strip down big Harleys and Indians, to make them more like flat track race bikes and more like the lighter, quicker British twins that many soldiers had seen "over there." One part of the customizing process was bobbing (shortening and lightening) the heavy steel fenders found on the American bikes.

Bobbers were modified by their owners (as were most early choppers). They set the stage for the more stylized and colorful – albeit less functional – choppers that followed. Nowadays, bobbers are back in fashion as customizers strive to build motorcycles unlike the soulless generic choppers produced like sausage on endless reality-TV spin offs.

Day 54:
Arlen Ness
Ness grew up surrounded by Southern California hot-rod culture but was always drawn to motorcycles. He did not buy his first motorcycle, a '47 Harley "knucklehead," until after he was married – using

money he won in bowling competitions! Ness customized that bike and it immediately attracted the attention of photographers and magazine editors. In those early days he couldn't afford new bikes to work on, so he recustomized that knucklehead over and over, and it appeared looking totally different in one magazine after another. That strategy built his reputation.

Ness was one of the first custom builders to realize that the advent of CNC machining allowed him to make short runs of custom parts that would have been almost impossible to build any other way. He created a successful custom-parts business that allowed him finance a series of wild customs, most of which he still owns.

Day 55:
Pierre Terreblanche

This South African followed Tamburini as chief designer at Ducati. He created the tiny, perfect Supermono production racer – a bike so gorgeous that, almost two decades after its limited production run, there are annual rumors that a street-legal version is about to enter mass production.

His detractors feel Terreblanche's 999 is ugly compared to the bike it replaced, Tamburini's 916. In fairness, Terreblanche's designs always look better in the metal than they do in pictures. The best things about his work, though, are that he seems not to care what things look like or what anyone thinks about them… and that people who own his bikes come to love them more and more. The revolutionary first-generation Multistrada was downright ugly until you'd ridden it a few thousand miles. Then it was beautiful.

Day 56:
Joint award: Peter Fonda and Dan "Grizzly Adams" Haggerty

Peter Fonda, who was an avid motorcyclist, wrote and produced the film Easy Rider. Fonda bought several surplus Los Angeles Police Department Harley-Davidsons to use in the movie. Two of these were used as the basis of the famous "Captain America" choppers required when filming. Although Fonda conceived the styling and modification of the bikes, most of the assembly was done by another actor-biker, Dan Haggerty (who later costarred with a grizzly bear on '70s TV.)

Two of the bikes, you ask? Yes, one was used in the riding scenes. That bike was intentionally wrecked in a stunt crash in the film. An identical machine was used for close-ups. It was stolen soon after the film's completion and never recovered. Fonda and Haggerty may have only collaborated on a single custom, but they managed to build the world's most recognizable motorcycle.

Day 57:
Hans Muth

As lead designer of the German design consultancy Target, Muth styled the Porsche 911 and BMW 2002 cars, along with several influential concept bikes. One of those made it into production as the now-collectible Suzuki Katana. Muth was also responsible for the striking looks of the BMW R90S.

Day 58:
Mike Corbin

Most of the custom bikes made in the U.S. have seats sewn by Corbin's company. But Mike Corbin has done more than cushion motorcyclists' butts. He's a free-thinking designer willing to take risks – some of which worked out, like the time he set the outright land speed record for an electric motorcycle. Others, like the daring Sparrow trike were creative successes but commercial failures.

Day 59:
Roland Sands

Sands' family owns Performance Machine, which has long been one of the largest suppliers of custom wheels and brakes to chopper builders. Many of the bikes that used PM wheels, ironically, didn't perform very well – they were built for looks only.

That didn't sit well with Sands, who was a very successful motorcycle racer. After retiring from the track, he has become a lone evangelist of customs that turn and stop as well as they look and go.

Dark Days

Motorcycling, as your mother likely told you, can be dangerous. Add to those inherent dangers the fact that the sport appeals to risk-takers who often extend their adventure-seeking into other areas of life and you've got a recipe for some dark days. To say nothing of the way motorcycle companies and organizations have historically been mismanaged. Indeed, for years it seemed the only time the mainstream media noticed us at all was when things had gone badly wrong. Here are nine such moments and one sad – though inspiring – tale of amazing courage.

Day 60:

"Murderdrome" board-track racing disaster (1912)

At the time, board tracks had "progressed" from short, gently banked bicycle tracks to longer and much steeper banked "motordromes." The faster tracks weren't just more dangerous for riders, they were dangerous for the fans too. On one such track in Newark NJ on Sept. 8th, Eddie "The Texas Cyclone" Hasha competed with five other riders in five-mile handicap race.

In the middle of the race, Hasha lost control and his motorcycle careened along the top rail, killing four young fans who'd been hanging over for a better view. Then it hit a post, killing Hasha and sending the bike caroming back down onto the track where another racer, Johnny Albright hit it. He too died. The newspapers began calling such tracks murderdromes and one by one, local authorities closed them. If there was a bright spot in any of this, it was that flat track racing was invented to replace the board tracks, but motorcycle racing was never again as popular a spectator sport in America.

Day 61:

The Death of T.E. Lawrence (1935)

Lawrence became renowned as "Lawrence of Arabia" after WWI and the publication of his epic memoir "Seven Pillars of Wisdom." He enlisted in the Royal Air Force under a pseudonym, and indulged in a great love affair with fast motorcycles, notably Brough Superiors. He died six days after crashing on a road in rural Dorset, in May, 1935.

Had Lawrence lived he would have been one of the most famous and dashing exponents of the sport. Instead, his death became the subject of conspiracy theories. Some felt he was killed by foreign agents, and others claimed he'd never died at all. The latter group thought he'd taken on a vital intelligence assignment in the Arab world. In fact, he was simply riding too fast, came upon a group of children on bicycles and lost control after swerving to avoid them.

Day 62:
Life Magazine's coverage of the Hollister "motorcycle riot" (1947)
A few hundred motorcyclists got rowdy in Hollister on the July 4th weekend. Townspeople admitted it had been no worse than what the cowboys did each year at the annual stock fair (and in fact the town staged motorcycle races in Hollister *again* just a few months later.)

A few days after the so-called riot, a photographer staged a photo of a beefy, threatening-looking drunk, slumped on a motorcycle surrounded by empty beer cans. Life Magazine ran in, triggering a media frenzy that lasted well into the 1960s. In a bizarre example of life imitating art, real gangs of motorcycle outlaws were formed in response to those stories.

Day 63:
Black Sunday (20th May, 1973)
Monza Circuit, outskirts of Milan, Italy: One of the 350 GP machines blew its motor and dumped a large

quantity of oil on the circuit. This was either not seen or worse, deliberately ignored by officials who wanted to keep the event running on schedule.

In the first lap of the 250cc race that followed, 17 riders crashed in the very fast first turn. Two of the greatest riders of the day, Jarno Saarinen and Renzo Pasolini, were instantly killed. A number of other riders were seriously injured, including Walter Villa who was resuscitated only with difficulty. Jarno Saarinen, in particular, was marked for greatness and there are many who still observe the date, May 20th as the worst day in the history of motorcycle racing.

Day 64:
Collapse of the British bike industry (c. 1980)
The Model T succeeded in killing off the U.S. motorcycle industry before anyone realized what had happened. But the British industry thrived until well into the 1960s when the men managing Velocette, Matchless, Norton, AJS, BSA and Triumph should have known better than to think, "We can keep doing business as usual," in the face of Japanese competition.

Instead of responding to the Japanese invasion by innovating – at a time when most of the world's motorcycle engineering knowledge was still based in Britain – the industry was hidebound from top to bottom. Managers didn't ride motorcycles themselves and were out of touch with real riders' needs and wants, and militant unions were dead set against updating manufacturing techniques to match Japanese quality and prices. By the early '80s, only Triumph was left and it too closed its doors in 1983.

Day 65:

R.I.P. Mike Hailwood (1981)

Giacomo Agostini seems hardly to have aged and is now the elder statesman of the great racers of the '60s and '70s. It is truly a shame that Mike Hailwood, the greatest rider of all time – a genuine hero with medals to prove it, as well as a kind, funny, modest man – is not alive to share Ago's long and honorable retirement.

Like Ago, Mike the Bike retired from motorcycle racing almost completely unscathed. He was killed driving home with a take-out order of fish and chips, when a truck suddenly attempted a U-turn on a dark and rainswept road. He was only 42 years old. His five year-old daughter also perished in the accident.

Day 66:

The end of the combined Grand National Championship (1985)

Until 1985, the American Motorcycle Association's Grand National Championship was unique in the world, in that racers accumulated points in road races as well as flat track races on mile, half-mile, and short tracks. Last but not least they competed in "TT" races with jumps. As a result, the AMA #1 plate holder could really lay claim to being the best all-round motorcycle racer in the world.

When Kenny Roberts went to Europe and became the first American ever to win the 500cc Grand Prix world championship, it was on the strength of his ability to control a sliding motorcycle

– a skill he learned racing the flat tracks back home.
Despite that object lesson in the benefits of a
combined series, the powers-that-be in the AMA
decided to split the championships into a separate
GNC for flat track only, and a road-racing series that
soon evolved into the AMA Superbike Championship.
The riders were never again as colorful, and the
championship(s) were never as interesting.

Day 67:
The repeal of mandatory helmet laws (1975-95)
Before 1966, no states required motorcycle riders to
wear crash helmets. That changed when the Highway
Safety Act forced states to enact helmet laws or lose a
portion of their federal highway funding. By 1975, 47
states required helmet use and not surprisingly,
motorcycle fatalities and serious head injuries
plummeted. However, in that year – and under
pressure from California legislators, as that state was
a holdout – Congress revisited the Highway Safety
Act and removed the language requiring crash
helmets. By 1980 more than half of the helmet laws
had been repealed.

Through the early '90s, there was a gradual
rise in the number of states requiring helmet use and
then, again, a change in the wording of federal
highway funding legislation precipitated another
spate of repeals. Now, only about 20 states require all
motorcyclists to wear helmets. Despite an
overwhelming safety argument in favor of helmet use
(riding a motorcycle without a helmet really *is* as
dangerous as your mom thinks it is!) half of all riders
will not do so unless threatened with a ticket.

Two notes from the Department of Irony: California – the state that broke the back of the original helmet legislation and triggered a landslide of helmet law repeals – now is one of the minority of states that *does* require all riders to wear at least this minimal protection. Four states do not even require children to wear helmets. One of them is New Hampshire. Their car license plates famously carry the slogan "Live free or die." Perhaps their motorcycle license plates should read, "Live free *and* die."

Day 68:
The premature death of John Britten (1995)
John Britten was a self-taught New Zealand engineer who made one of the most fantastic motorcycles ever, the Britten V1000 twin-cylinder racer. It was one of the fastest motorcycles of the early '90s, packed with amazing and innovative technology that could only have come from someone completely outside mainstream motorcycle design. Britten's achievement was even more impressive when one considers that the motorcycles were made essentially by hand, in a shed in New Zealand, by a very small team of (usually very stoned) enthusiasts.

There was a constant flow of rumors in the early '90s about what Britten would do next – when Harley-Davidson built its ill-fated VR-1000 superbike there were many who asked, "Why on earth didn't they just hire John Britten?" Then there were rumors that a new Indian company had contracted Britten to design both a race bike and a street bike. Whatever he would have done, it would have been great. Sadly, he died very suddenly, at age 45 of an aggressively malignant melanoma. For more on this fascinating man, read "John Britten" his biography, by Tim Hanna.

Day 69:
The Mont Blanc Tunnel Fire (1999)
This is one of the longest and highest tunnels in the world, connecting the highway systems of France and Italy through the Alps. When a transport truck caught fire in the middle of the tunnel, the smoke and flames trapped about 50 people. Of those 12 survived. All of them reached the mouth of the tunnel saying, "That guy on the motorcycle saved my life."

That man was Pier Lucio Tinazzi, an Italian tunnel employee who rode his BMW K75 in and out of the tunnel – a seven-mile round trip through choking smoke and fumes – to bring people out. On the final trip, he came across an unconscious driver who he could not get onto the back of his motorcycle. He refused to abandon him and dragged him to shelter in a small room off the tunnel. Both men died.

Tinazzi was posthumously awarded Italy's highest honor for civilian bravery, as well as the Federation Internationale Motocycliste (FIM's) gold medal for exceptional courage and service to the sport of motorcycling. Every year, several hundred Italian motorcyclists ride to the tunnel mouth on the anniversary of Tinazzi's heroic deed.

Ultimate Races

Great battles make great races – so you can see compelling races at unheralded club meets if you happen to catch a duel between closely matched amateurs. And any round of any AMA professional championship, whether it's supercross, motocross, superbikes or Grand National flat track racing is a spectacle.

That said, there are some annual events that combine a historic and particularly challenging track with a perennially strong field. Here are ten events that will never disappoint.

Day 70:
The United States Grand Prix at Laguna Seca
The USGP had a checkered history for years. It was briefly part of Daytona's Speed Week in the '60s and after many years without a U.S. round of the world championships it returned to Laguna Seca in the early '90s. Kenny Roberts promoted some of those races but gave up when it proved impossible to make any money at them.

Over the winter of 2004-'05 Yamaha spent several million dollars at the track, funding improvements that again made Laguna Seca eligible for FIM certification. Thanks to Yamaha and sponsorship by Red Bull, America again had a Grand Prix in 2005. Now, it is a July fixture on the MotoGP calendar.

Despite heavy traffic and some challenges finding accommodation for 100,000 fans in tiny Monterey, California, and despite competition from Indy and now Austin, Laguna Seca is *the* American motorcycle race. The track is spectacular and if you're willing to walk it offers many great fan viewpoints. Just make sure you get to the hillside overlooking the famous Corkscrew turn early!

Laguna Seca is administered by a charitable foundation called SCRAMP (Sports Car Racing Association of the Monterey Peninsula.) Contact them for ticket and scheduling information at: www.laguna-seca.com or by telephoning 800-327 7322.

Day 71:
The Isle of Man Tourist Trophy
There is an entire chapter of this book devoted to the TT. Practice and racing take place over a two-week period in late May and early June. Nothing you will ever see (or hear) compares to a superbike traveling at full speed, often just a few feet away from you, as it races down building- and tree-lined roads. In places, the course is narrower than some American driveways.

Many motorcycle fans have the impression that it's impossible to find accommodation on the island during the TT. Nothing could be further from the truth, as thousands of Manx residents open their homes to visitors. If you want to get a motorcycle to the island, you'll need to use some ingenuity as ferries are heavily booked, but it can be done. No tickets are required to watch the races.

You should begin planning your TT trip a year or more ahead. Start by visiting the excellent www.iomtt.com website.

Day 72:
The Springfield Mile

In the old days, the national flat track champion was the winner of a single race, the Springfield Mile. Nowadays, the all-American, good-'ole-boy stars of GNC racing come to Springfield early in the season and again on the Labor Day weekend. Both events are doubleheaders, with a TT race the night before the mile, so there are actually four GNC races at Springfield.

The Mile race is held on the smooth, fast Illinois State Fairgrounds horse track. It's a tactical drafting battle with packs of riders coming past the grandstand wheel-to-wheel and bar-to-bar at 140 miles an hour.

Day 73:
Anaheim Supercross

Like NASCAR, the most-watched and most prestigious race of the AMA Supercross Championship is the first one. "Anaheim I" is traditionally held in early January. In recent years the event has completely sold out Angel Stadium – something the baseball team never does – so a second round, cleverly called "Anaheim II," has been added later in January. Everyone who's anyone in the motorcycle business seems to show up there. It's not uncommon to see MotoGP stars and motorcycle company presidents wandering in the concourse.

Day 74:

MotoGP or World Superbikes in Assen, Holland

While you could argue that any Spanish round of the MotoGP world championships or any British World Superbike round has more rabid fans, who needs rabies?

The Dutch track at Assen is one of the most challenging and historic venues in world-championship racing. The MotoGP round (traditionally held in late June) and the World Superbike Championship round (early September) are both attended by huge crowds that are particularly fun-loving. For more information go to www.tt-assen.com.

Day 75:

AMA Superbikes at Road Atlanta

Over the last few years, the AMA Superbike championship has evolved to the point where most of the tracks on the schedule are pretty good, both from the rider's (mainly safety) perspective and in terms of fan amenities. While improving rider safety is always good, some old-time fans begrudge the stop-and-go nature of most new tracks, where a superbike can't even use top gear.

Safe, technical, stop-and-go racing is not what you'll see at Road Atlanta. Its fast downhill Turn 12 is the most hair-raising turn remaining in American racing and it is worth the price of admission all by itself. More information and tickets are available on line at www.roadatlanta.com or by calling 800-849 7223.

Day 76:
World Championship Motocross at Namur

The Belgians may not have invented motocross (or beer, for that matter) but both motocross and beer have certainly found their adopted homes there. The motocross track at Namur, on the grounds of an actual castle, is the site of the annual Belgian MXGP in early September. The setting, history and passion of the fans make this *the* international motocross event.

The Belgian sense of humor, beer with up to 14% alcohol and French fries that are so good you'll make a meal of them are all other great reasons to attend. Information is available from the Belgian equivalent of our AMA. Reach them at www.fmb-bmb.be.

Day 77:
The Baja 1000

America's premiere desert race is not held in America at all – it's the SCORE Baja 1000, held on Mexico's Baja peninsula. The good news for fans is that you don't need a ticket to see it. The bad news is that even though the race is now laid out in a loop most years (it used to always be a point-to-point course the length of the peninsula) you'll still only see each competitor pass by once.

The ultimate fan experience at Baja is not to be a fan at all, but to join someone's pit crew. This is easier than you'd think, as the race is open to all comers and many competitors arrive in Ensenada short of help. The race takes place in November. Check out: www.score-international.com.

Get on track!

There are dozens of race-tracks in the U.S. and hundreds of groups that rent them for track days. Getting on track is fun and a great way to improve your riding and test your limits without risking your license (or life) on the street.

Don't worry if you're not a racer – all you need is a reasonable set of leathers, a good helmet, boots and gloves, and a good attitude. You don't need to have a "track-prepped" hardcore sport bike. As long as your motorcycle has good tires and isn't leaking, you can tape over the lights and remove the mirrors (that's often all that's required) right at the track.

Every reputable track day operator splits riders into slow, medium and fast groups so you needn't worry about being blitzed by fearless teenagers on their Yamazuki crotch rockets. If it's your first time on the track, organizers will always find a local expert to show you the proper lines. Most of the time, the promise of a beer at the end of the day is enough to encourage someone from the fast group to keep an eye on you and provide a little one-on-one coaching.

The following is a list of great tracks you can ride, with one selected track day organizer's contact information for each. This information was current when I researched it.

The organizers on this list are reliable and have been in business long enough to know what they're doing. However dates at most of these tracks are also offered by other companies. Since schedules change all the time, you may want to check an up-to-date list on the internet. Two good ones are found at www.sportrider.com and www.roadracingworld.com. Their print parents, Sport Rider Magazine and Roadracing World Magazine are also good references for track days.

Day 78:
Laguna Seca
One of America's greatest and most historic tracks, located in Monterey, California about two hours south of San Francisco. Note that there are strict noise rules here. If your motorcycle has an aftermarket exhaust it will almost certainly be too loud and you will not be allowed to ride. Reinstall your stock muffler before going. (Track information: www.laguna-seca.com, 831-242 8201)
Track Days:
Keigwins@theTrack
www.keigwin.com
650-949 5609

Day 79:
Barber Motorsports Park
New and beautiful. A technical flowing layout that is easy for beginners to enjoy but has enough challenge for experts, too. (Track information: www.barbermotorsports.com, 205-298 9040)
Track Days:
Fastrack Riders
www.fastrackriders.com/877-560 2233

Day 80:

Infineon Raceway

Just north of the Bay Area, in scenic Napa Valley. Not as famous as Laguna Seca (and with the aesthetic challenges that attend all 'dragstrip' tracks) Infineon is every bit as challenging and technical as 'the dry lake'. (Track information: www.infineonraceway.com, 800-870 RACE)

Track Days:

Keigwins@theTrack

www.keigwin.com

650-949 5609

Day 81:

Road America

This long (four-mile) track in Elkhart Lake, WI serves the Chicagoland metro area. (Track information: www.roadamerica.com, 800-365 RACE)

Track Days:

Northeast Sportbike Association

www.nesba.com

877-286 3722

Day 82:

Virginia International Raceway

A beautiful and underrated track that's ideally suited to motorcycles. Located right on the VA-NC border. (Track information: www.virclub.com, 434-822 7700)

Track Days:

Northeast Sportbike Association

www.nesba.com

877-286 3722

Day 83:
Mid-Ohio Sports Car Course
The first part of the name is accurate, it's smack in the middle of Ohio. The second part is a little misleading as there are now more motorcycle races here than there are car races. Recently repaved and refurbished. (Track information: 800-MID OHIO)
Track Days:
Sportbike Track Time
www.sportbiketracktime.com
419-822 0350

Day 84:
Miller Motorsports Park
A state of the art facility recently opened near Salt Lake City. The track accepts members or visitors, although visitors must attend a two-hour orientation. (Track information: www.millermotorsportspark.com, 801-563 4262)
Track Days:
Miller Motorsports Park Open Track Days
www.millermotorsportspark.com/opentrackdays.cfm
801-563 4250

Day 85:
Willow Springs Raceway
This fast, challenging track is located in the hot, windy high desert about an hour east of Los Angeles on terrain that, if it wasn't used for a race track, would be a great place for gangsters to dump bodies. "The Streets of Willow" is a slower track, also on the property, that frequently holds track days as well.

'The Streets' is a little less intimidating for beginners.
(Track information: www.willowspringsraceway.com,
661-256 6666)
Track Days:
Pacific Track Time
www.pacifictracktime.com
530-223 0622

Day 86:
New Hampshire International Speedway
NHIS replaced the much-loved but outdated Bryar
track in 1990. In the late '90s, NHIS got an unfair
reputation for being dangerous. It's not pretty but it
serves an important purpose as the closest track to the
big northeast population centers. It's about an hour
and a half north of Boston. (Track information:
www.nhis.com, 603-783 4744)
Track Days:
Team Pro-Motion
www.teampromotion.com
215-671 8660

Isle of Man Trivia

The Isle of Man TT is truly a race (actually, a whole week of racing) that every motorcyclist needs to see at least once in a lifetime. Of course, many of the thousands of fans who travel to the Island do so every year. If you want to pretend you're not a newcomer, you'll need to know a few bits of island trivia. This should get you off to a good start…

Day 87:
How **many corners???**
Depending on who's counting, there are about 140 corners or bends on the 37.73-mile "Mountain" course. Of those, nearly 70 have names and knowing them is one of the keys to making sense of this long, long race – indeed, learning the place names is an important stage in memorizing the course for racers, too. It's all made more confusing by the fact that many names are in the old Manx Gaelic language. The long straightaway called Cronk-y-Voddy, for example, means "hill of dogs."

Day 88:
It wasn't always "The Mountain Course"
Since 1911, most TT races have been held on the current course, over Mount Snaefel. However, from 1907-1910 the races were held on west side of the

island, on the 15.8-mile "St. John's" course. Between 1955-'60 some 125cc and 250cc races were held on the 10.75-mile "Clypse" course.

Day 89:
First lap at over 100mph
In 1955, everyone expected Geoff Duke to lap the "Mountain" circuit at over 100 miles an hour. During the third lap of the '55 Senior, announcers reported he'd lapped in 22 minutes and 39 seconds – exactly 100mph. The Grandstand erupted in spontaneous cheers. Minutes later, red-faced ACU officials discovered a rounding-off error. Geoff Duke had in fact only achieved 99.97 mph.

Day 90:
No, *really*. The first lap over 100mph
In 1957, Bob McIntyre set the first 100 hundred mile an hour lap. And the second. And the third and fourth. He was riding a four-cylinder Gilera. That race was also noteworthy as one of the rare appearances of the Moto Guzzi V-*eight* 500cc Grand Prix bikes.

Day 91:
Tyn-what?
The Isle of Man is the world's oldest democracy. The Manx parliament, called the "Tynwald" has been in continuous operation since 979 A.D. For centuries, the parliament met on a hill called – brace yourself – "Tynwald Hill." It now meets in a building in Douglas, but the hill's still there, just west of Ballacraine Corner.

Day 92:
Who's "yer maun"?
Joey Dunlop's record of 26 TT victories, between 1977 and 2000 will likely never be broken. He was known to his legion of Irish fans simply as, "yer maun." Thing to say when, in a Manx pub, someone makes a comment about a racer you've never heard of: "Aye, but there will never be another like Joey."

Day 93:
There was never a Kate at "Kate's Cottage"
There's a tight left turn just as riders come down off the mountain. It's known around the world as "Kate's Cottage." Indeed, there is a white cottage marking the spot. However, it belonged to a family named Tate. Years ago an excited Manx Radio commentator mispronounced the name, and it's been Kate's ever since.

Day 94:
Those guys in orange vests aren't roadworkers
Occasionally during a TT practice session, you'll see a rider wearing a high-visibility orange vest over his leathers. That vest indicates that the rider is "newcomer," competing in the TT for the first time. Newcomers are also given a small time "allowance" in qualifying – usually 30 seconds. However, if they need that allowance to qualify, they must wear the orange vest in the race.

Day 95:

If you're going to claim another race is your favorite...

Although the TT is the Isle of Man's internationally famous race, there are races for amateurs and vintage motorcycles on the Mountain course at the end of the summer. The atmosphere for these races, dubbed the Manx Grand Prix is more relaxed, the crowds at the pubs and restaurants are a little smaller and the racing is really just as spectacular.

America's World Center of Racing: Daytona Beach

Every American racer dreams of winning the Daytona 200 and for much of its history it was the only American motorcycle race that attracted truly worldwide interest. Ironically, every March hundreds of thousands of people come to Daytona for Bike Week and don't watch the races. If you're one of those people, here are the ten things you need to know to appreciate the Daytona racing scene.

Day 96:
It used to take true grit to set a record
Long before there was a Daytona International Speedway, races and record attempts were held on the sandy beachfronts of Daytona and neighboring Ormond, Florida.

At low tide the damp, hard-packed sand provided a straight, dead level surface that ran for miles. It was perfect for land-speed record attempts. In 1904, the pioneering aviator Glenn H. Curtiss rode his two-cylinder motorcycle 67.36 mph – a class record that stood for seven years.

In 1907, Curtiss returned to the beach with a motorcycle powered by one of his V-8 airplane engines. That motorcycle made about 40 horsepower – a heck of lot in the day. It reached a speed of 136.27 mph.

Curtiss' V-8 wasn't just the world's fastest motorcycle – it was the fastest thing on wheels, period. The daring young man held the land speed record for twelve years until Ralph dePalma went faster in a Packard car, also on Daytona Beach. That was the last time that the outright land speed record was ever held by a motorcycle.

Day 97:
It could've been *Miami* International Speedway
If Daytona really is "the world center of racing" it's thanks to Bill France Sr., who built Daytona International Speedway (and was the founder of NASCAR). France was a mechanic in Virginia and Maryland in the '30s. Winters up there made working on cars in poorly heated garages miserable, so he decided to move to Miami. His car broke down at Daytona and he liked it so much he stayed. He joined in the local beach races, then became a race promoter. He built the Speedway in '59. The AMA moved the 200-mile National Championship from the beach to his track in '61.

Day 98:
A race with lots of class(es)
The Daytona 200 has long been America's biggest motorcycle race, but like everything at Speedway, the "200" is completely controlled by the France family, who still own the track. They've changed the rules on many occasions – often to the dismay of fans, racers, and even the American Motorcycle Association.

From 1937-'76 the race was run under AMA Class C rules. Until 1968, Class C permitted overhead valve motors of up to 500cc and side valve motors (the type used by Harley-Davidson) of up to 750cc. In '69 the AMA allowed all Class C machines to displace 750cc, effectively ending Harley-Davidson's ability to compete.

From '77-'84 the race was for Formula 1 motorcycles – typically 750cc two-strokes like the Yamaha TZ750. When race fans were bored by years of Yamaha domination, the France family arbitrarily made the 200 a race for a new class of production-based racers called "Superbikes".

It was a Superbike race from 1985 to 2004, when the Jimmy France announced another class change. Beginning in 2005, the 200 would be a race for Formula Extreme-class motorcycles. The reason: they wanted the race to be run under rules that would again allow a Harley-Davidson (aka Buell) to be competitive.

Day 99:
"Win on Sunday, sell (wait a minute – *Hondas?*) on Monday"
In 1970, BSA, Triumph, Norton and Honda all had new, bet-the-company 750cc motorcycles hitting the market. A win was such a vital part of BSA's business plan that the company even lured Mike Hailwood out of retirement to ride a new Rocket III in the "200". Even Harley-Davidson had an all-new XR750 racer for Cal Rayborn. Virtually all of the factory bikes broke down in the race but at the end of the day all anyone remembered was that the last Honda running was the one Dick Mann rode to victory.

That was the first time that any motorcycle not

made in the U.S. or Britain ever won the 200. It gave Honda's new 750-Four instant credibility and crippled sales of big British bikes. It was the last battle in the "Japanese invasion" of the U.S. motorcycle market and the Japanese won.

Day 100:
Supercross was invented here
In 1972, someone had the bright idea of building an artificial track in the Daytona infield for a round of the AMA's motocross championship. The Speedway hired Gary Bailey to design the course. That race is generally considered the first Supercross race. Two years later the AMA conducted its first full (three-round!) Supercross championship and the first of those races, too, was held in the Daytona infield.

Day 101:
That's *Mister* Daytona, to you
Scott Russell and Miguel Duhamel have each won the Daytona 200 five times. Russell gets the nod as "Mister Daytona" because all of his wins came on Superbike-class machinery. Russell nearly won seven of the races; he also finished second in two races where the combined margin of victory totaled only .06 seconds.

Two of Russell's wins were on Yamaha motorcycles. The "tuning forkers" won the race 18 times. The only other manufacturer that comes close is Harley-Davidson with 16 wins, most of them on the sand.

Day 102:
That was close!
The smallest margin of victory ever was Miguel
Duhamel's 0.01-second advantage over Scott Russell
in 1996. Duhamel has another claim to fame that no
one else can come close to matching: he won his first
"200" in 1991 and his fifth in 2005 – a fourteen year
span.

Day 103:
If I see one more Harley, I'll…
A trip to Main Street during Bike Week will remind
you that, in America "Motorcycle" = "Harley-
Davidson". If you come for the races and want a night
time dose of sport bike culture, forget biker bars near
the beach. Head for the Hess garage just west of I-5
on International Speedway Boulevard. If you come on
your own bike, feel free to bet on an illegal street race
– just make sure you bet on <u>losing</u>. These guys are
<u>serious</u>.

Day 104:
Talk the talk
To create the impression you're a seasoned Bike
Week veteran, say, "I miss the old North Turn bar,"
when you're buying a round. In its original
incarnation, the North Turn was a down-at-the-heels
dive, located at the north end of the old beach course.
Although it's still there, it's evolved into a tourist trap
– a "Bubba Gump's" for the leather set during Bike
Week, and one of a thousand generic NASCAR-
themed sports bars the rest of the year. If you must
go, it's located on the A1A highway in Ponce Inlet.

Day 105:
Walk the walk to the old beach monument
If you can stand the bright morning sunlight outside –
and the sound of waves crashing inside your head –
the beach is a great place to walk off a Bikeweek
hangover (and oh, you'll have one.) No pilgrimage to
Daytona is complete without a visit to the beach
monument to early "200" racers. It's located across
from 100 N. Atlantic Avenue.

The greatest road racers of the last 50 years

In a century of motorcycle racing, there have obviously been more than ten great stars. Looking back from the present day, it is difficult to rank stars from the postwar era like Geoff Duke; the bikes they raced were underpowered by modern standards but their tires offered far less grip, and they were racing on far more dangerous tracks. If it's hard to extrapolate back past the 1950s, it's impossible to rate pioneer racers like the charismatic Jacques "Jake" deRosier. In the modern era, however, the following ten racers were certainly among the very best.

Day 106:
Stanley Michael Bailey Hailwood

Hailwood could have been a spoiled rich kid competing with daddy's money. His father, after all, was the owner of King's of Oxford – a very successful chain of British motorcycle dealerships. Despite that advantage, it was hard not to like the man who came to be known around the world as "Mike the Bike." He was funny, handsome and he threw great parties; his apartment near London's Heathrow airport was a hangout for many of England's best jazz musicians. Most importantly he was very, very fast.

Hailwood was born in 1940 and started racing at 17, an age that was young at the time. He quickly started winning races, and before his career was over he'd won 76 Grands Prix and nine World Championships. Hailwood's rivalry with Giacomo Agostini illuminated Grand Prix racing in the mid-'60s. There are many people who feel that period was the sport's greatest era.

Day 107:
Valentino Rossi

Valentino Rossi's career is not over, but the Italian known as "The Doctor" has already firmly established himself as one of greatest racers of all time. Rossi is the son of Graziano Rossi, who was a world-class racer in the '70s.

Rossi was only 17 when he won his first World Championship (1997) in the 125cc class. He won the 250cc title in '99 and the final 500cc title in 2001. After that, the Federation Internationale Motocyclist changed the rules of the top racing class and it became known as "MotoGP." Rossi won the first four years of that championship, too.

Besides his obvious talent, he was famous for his post-race victory laps, which involved elaborate costumes and props smuggled onto the track by his rabid fans. Such behavior drove race organizers crazy but since Rossi was by far the highest-paid racer of all time, the fines are a small price to pay.

Day 108:
Joey Dunlop
Dunlop, born in Northern Ireland in 1952, was
without question the most successful "real roads"
racer of all time. His record of 26 Isle of Man TT
wins will stand forever. In addition, he won literally
hundreds of other races and was the (motorcycle) F1
World Champion every year from 1982-'86.

"Yer maun" (as he was known to his Irish
fans) was a taciturn guy who kept his own council
and did not suffer fools gladly. He was an old-school
racer – though he was world famous, he was happiest
when left alone in the pits to tinker on his own bikes.

After Yugoslavia collapsed into civil war in
the early '90s, Dunlop filled his race transporter with
medical supplies and without any fanfare or publicity,
drove across Europe and into the war zone, to deliver
his cargo to embattled hospitals. He was awarded the
MBE (Member of the British Empire) for his
motorcycle racing exploits and the OBE (Order of the
British Empire) for his humanitarian work. He died in
a racing accident in Talinn, Estonia in 2000.

Day 109:
Giacomo Agostini
"Ago" was born in 1942. He started racing in
hillclimb events on the mountainous roads around
Bergamo (Italy) where he lived.

Agostini's record of 122 Grand Prix wins is
another mark that will stand forever. Most of Ago's
wins came on MV Agusta motorcycles, which were
the two-wheeled "Ferraris" of their day. Indeed if
there's an asterisk on his record, it's that he made

winning look too easy – his bikes were often far superior to anyone else's, and in 17 years of racing he never had a serious crash.

Usually when someone's described as having "movie-star good looks" it's just a figure of speech but in Ago's case it was literally true. After he retired, he flirted with a film career in his native Italy. He remains a great ambassador for the sport of motorcycle racing and still draws plenty of fans to his numerous public appearances.

Day 110:
Kenny Roberts
Roberts was born in Modesto, California on the last day of 1951. That was the only time he was late to any finish line. He won the first AMA Grand National event he ever entered. He went on to win the Grand National Championship in '73 and '74 (when AMA racers still competed on both dirt and pavement.)

The brash American took his sliding, flat track style to Europe in the late '70s. He won the 500cc World Championship three years in a row ending in 1980. Along the way he threatened to promote a rival championship, that he dubbed the "World Series". That threat resulted in better pay and safety for racers. After retiring as a racer, he won several World Championships as a team manager. His son Kenny Roberts Junior was a world champ himself, riding for Suzuki in 2000

Day 111:
Jarno Saarinen
We'll never know just how great the "Flying Finn" might have been. In 1971 Saarinen served notice of his potential when he finished second in the 250cc World Championship and third in the 350cc class on non-factory equipment.

In '72, Yamaha signed him to its factory team and he won his only World Championship, in the 250cc class. Three races into the 1973 season, Saarinen was leading in both the 250cc and 500cc classes when he was tragically killed.

Saarinen got his start as an ice racer in his native Finland. The spiked tires used in that sport allow racers lean their bikes at extreme angles when cornering. Saarinen took the same fearless approach as a road racer and was the first person to intentionally drag a knee when cornering.

Day 112:
Freddie Spencer
"Fast Freddie" was born in Lousiana in 1961. He started racing at 5 and continued to race at every opportunity until he was a teenager, frequently competing in dirt track and road races on the same weekend or even the same day. He was only 17 when he won his first AMA National.

In 1980, Spencer rode for Honda in the still-developing AMA Superbike class. His battles with the great Eddie Lawson helped turn Superbikes into the premier racing class in the U.S. In 1983, he won the 500cc World Championship. In 1985, he won three classes at Daytona, including the Daytona 200 before returning to Europe and winning both the 250cc and 500cc World Championships. He won his final AMA Superbike race in 1995, sixteen years after he won his first.

Day 113:
Cal Rayborn
Rayborn was born in San Diego in 1940. As a teenager, he worked as a motorcycle courier in Southern California. He said the job taught him to ride fast, because the more deliveries he made, the more money he earned.

He won the '68 and '69 Daytona 200 races while riding for the Harley-Davidson factory team. His skill as a road racer earned him a spot in the 1972 Trans-Atlantic Match Races, which pitted the best American riders against the best of the British. His employers, however, did not want to supply him with a bike for the events. He borrowed an out-of-date, iron-barrel Harley XR and still managed to win three of the six races. For the first time, the Grand Prix stars of Europe were forced to admit that Americans could do more than race on dirt ovals.

Prior to the 1973 season, Rayborn decided that his future was as a road racing specialist and that he needed modern equipment. He signed with Suzuki and went to New Zealand over the winter, so he could practice on the unfamiliar machines. He was killed there in a racing accident.

Day 114:
Michael Doohan
"Mick" Doohan entered the 500cc class at a time when it featured a great depth of talent – Wayne Rainey, Kevin Schwantz, Eddie Lawson and Wayne Gardner to name a few. In 1992 he suffered a serious leg injury and did not regain full fitness for a couple of years. By the time Doohan won the first of his five consecutive World Championships in '94, Rainey had been the victim of a career-ending crash, Lawson and Gardner had retired, and Schwantz was hampered by the cumulative effect of his own numerous crashes.

As a result, some felt that Doohan dominated the 500cc class through a lack of worthy opponents. Nothing could be further from the truth. Unlike Agostini, who was usually alone on clearly superior equipment, Doohan was one of five riders on factory Honda NSR500s. No less a rider than Valentino Rossi once said, "I've seen some of Mick's data readouts and fuck, he was very fast. It was him that made the difference, not the bike."

Day 115:
Barry Sheene
This South London kid may "only" have won two World Championships, but his cockney accent and ability to shrug off horrific injuries (you'll read about him elsewhere in this book under the heading 'Amazing Comebacks') appealed to millions of male fans.

His boyish good looks and infectious humor appealed to women, too. That combination attracted sponsors, including lots of companies that never

sponsored another racer before or after "Bazza".
Sheene was a heavy smoker. He even drilled a hole
through the chin bar of his helmet so he could have a
cigarette on the starting grid.

He died of cancer, aged 52.

Dirty but never down – the best riders who never needed pavement

It's even harder to choose the best off-road riders of all time, since "off-road" is not a single discipline. Even motocross tracks vary greatly between the gnarly U.S. tracks and the more freeway-esque European layouts. When you add in radically different sports ranging from trials – which takes place at walking speed – to Grand National flat tracks where speeds can reach 140 miles an hour, choosing the top ten is a real challenge. However, I'm writing this book so I get to choose! Here are a double handful of guys who've all proven their ability to grab a handful of throttle and twist it, with no pavement in sight.

Day 116:
Ricky Carmichael – Best modern/American SX-MX rider

The world of motocross changed in two dramatic ways in the 1970s and '80s. First, the best riders and stiffest competition moved from Europe to the U.S., then the evolution of long-travel suspension changed riding styles and course design. MX and moreso SX came to emphasize rhythm and jumping. In the modern era, no rider can possibly challenge Ricky Carmichael's record. It is almost impossible even to summarize it – 13 national championships, well over 100 national race wins and two undefeated *seasons* in national motocross are just some of the highlights.

Day 117:

Scott Parker – winningest flat track rider

If they can call major league baseball's championship the *World* Series, we can call the AMA Grand National Championship the world championship of flat track racing. There are plenty of flat track fans who will want to punch me in the nose for not saying Flint, Michigan's Jay Springsteen was the best flat tracker of all time.

Despite the fragility of my nose, that title goes to another Flint native, Scott Parker. In his 22-year career, Parker won an untouchable nine championships and 94 national races. Between '94 and '98 he won five titles in a row. During that period he was totally dominant, with 39 race victories.

Day 118:

Roger DeCoster – Best European MX rider

This Belgian completely dominated open-class motocross in Europe throughout the 1970s, winning five 500cc world championships and countless victories in Trophee des Nations and Motocross des Nations competitions. This was the last period in which European motocross was clearly more competitive than the U.S. scene, as evidenced by DeCoster's many Trans-AMA championships.

Day 119:

Dougie Lampkin - Best trials rider

Almost beyond argument as the best trials rider of all time and certainly the best of the modern era. Between 1997 and 2003, Lampkin won seven outdoor

world championships and four indoor titles. Truly, the
things he can do on a motorcycle are impossible.

Day 120:
Stephane Peterhansel – master of the Paris-Dakar
The toughest off road race is, without doubt, the
Paris-Dakar. While the start and finish points are not
always Paris and Dakar, the course south through the
Sahara and central Africa was always utterly grueling.
Peterhansel is the undisputed master of this race,
having won it five times. He also won the world
enduro championship in 1997 and is a multi-time
ISDE class champion.

Day 121:
Chris Carr – the Prince of Peoria
Only Scott Parker has won more AMA national flat
track races than Carr. The compact Carr has won on
every type of flat track but has proven particularly
dominant at TT-style races (which include both left
and right turns and jumps.) His string of victories at
the popular Peoria TT earned him the nickname "the
Prince of Peoria." Carr has twice left the AMA Grand
National Championship. The first time was to race the
Harley-Davidson VR1000 superbike in the AMA
Superbike championship. The Harley was not
competitive enough to win but Carr was impressive
on it. He also won the short-lived Formula USA flat
track championship before returning to the GNC and
winning five straight titles.

Day 122:
Bob Hannah – motocross tough guy
The 17th century philosopher Thomas Hobbes said that without society the life of man would be "nasty, brutish, and short." He may as well have been describing Bob "Hurricane" Hannah. Of note is the fact that he won six AMA national championships in the '70s. A string of injuries kept him from winning overall titles in the '80s, but he was a member of the winning U.S. MX des Nations team in 1987 – making him one of the few riders to ride at the top level on both short and long-travel suspension motorcycles.

Day 123:
Jeremy McGrath – Gifted
McGrath is the all-time leader in national supercross wins (72), consecutive wins (13, tied with Ricky Carmichael) and wins in a single season (14, also tied with RC.) Although McGrath did not train as hard or maintain the supreme fitness level of other top MX riders, he made up for it with the ability to ride effortlessly.

Day 124:
Larry Roeseler – boss of the Baja
Winner of over twenty Baja 500 and 1000 races and a 10-time ISDE gold medalist. Roeseler nearly earned a spot on the "all-round" list by retiring from motorcycle competition and promptly winning the Baja 1000 on four wheels.

Day 125:

Juha Salminen – Ten times world enduro champ
Growing up in Finland Salminen showed excellent promise in both trials and motocross. However, he chose to focus on enduros. Almost from beginning, it was a field in which he had no equals. Salminen won 10 world championships before his sponsors asked him to move to the U.S. and compete here. After his arrival he had an almost perfect record in AMA GNCC enduros.

Great rivals and epic battles

The history of motorcycle racing is, in many ways, the history of great rivals. Six of the items on this list are memorable battles between worthy opponents, either in a single race or over a season. Two of the items on this list are battles between a rider and a particularly unforgiving track. One is a battle between a rider and his own machine and in one, the rider's only opposition was himself.

What do all the races on this list have in common? Well, you wish you'd been there to see them – and if you *were* lucky enough to see any of these incredible races, you'll never forget it.

Day 126:
Hailwood versus Agostini – 1966 and '67 Grand Prix seasons

Honda desperately wanted to wrest the 500cc Grand Prix championship from MV Agusta. The Japanese company already had a powerful motor but couldn't seem to make a suitable chassis for it. Moreover, its first foray into Formula One car racing was stretching the engineering department thin. Rather than attempt to build an all-new bike, Honda poached MV's star rider: Mike Hailwood. MV let Hailwood go and promoted their "junior" rider, Giacomo Agostini, who had spent 1965 as Mike's understudy.

Mike's smooth style allowed him to ride bikes that bucked and slid underneath him. He wasn't a complainer, either. He'd ride the wheels off anything he was given. He managed to win three races on the Honda 500 in '66 and five races in '67. But for the first time, even he couldn't make winning look easy. Mike used to climb off the Honda with his hands blistered and bleeding.

By contrast, Ago lacked Mike's raw talent but was a master of bike set-up. Mike won a few battles but Ago won the wars, taking the 500cc title in both years before Honda withdrew from Grands Prix in frustration.

Day 127:
Spencer versus Roberts – 1983 Swedish Grand Prix

Between them, Fast Freddie and King Kenny won every race that year. In the penultimate round, in Sweden, Roberts led going into the final turn. He left his braking to the absolute last moment but Spencer still dove up the inside to pass. Spencer had intentionally carried too much speed into the turn and the two riders bumped as Spencer pushed them both onto the grass at high speed. Spencer won and Roberts is still angry about it to this day.

As a result of that pass, all Spencer had to do win Honda's first 500cc world championship was finish right behind Roberts in the final race. Roberts won that one but Spencer took the title. Roberts then retired from competition and became a team manager.

Day 128:

The 1975 Indianapolis Mile

Kenny Roberts had been frustrated that his Yamaha-powered flat tracker was nowhere near as fast on mile tracks as the Harleys. Then Kel Carruthers stuffed a four-cylinder TZ750 road racing motor in a flat track frame. The bike had far too much power even for Roberts. Carruthers had to rig it with a "kill switch" that shut off one of the cylinders, or it would spin the rear tire all the way down the straightaways. Still, the one time Roberts rode it, he won on it.

That was at the 1975 Indy Mile. After wrestling with it the entire race, Roberts somehow found traction coming off the very last turn. The bike shot down the track and Roberts passed a shocked Jay Springsteen a few feet before the finish line. After the race, he blurted, "They don't pay me enough to ride that thing!" He needn't have worried, the AMA soon banned it.

Day 129:

Roberts versus Sheene – 1979 Grand Prix season

Kenny Roberts took the 500cc world championship from Barry Sheene in his first season in Grand Prix racing. He was the favorite to repeat as winner the next year but was badly injured in a preseason testing crash and missed the first round.

Sheene won that first race and felt confident of the season ahead but against all odds, Roberts came back to win the second round. For the rest of the season, Roberts battled the lingering effect of his injury while Sheene suffered from a few mechanical problems. With two races to go, the championship battle moved to Silverstone.

That British Grand Prix was one of the best races ever. Roberts and Sheene traded the lead almost every lap. Roberts won by a fraction of a second and won the overall championship that year, thoroughly demoralizing Sheene.

Day 130:
Edwards versus Bayliss – Imola, 2002 World Superbike Championship

Troy Bayliss had opened up an early-season lead but Colin Edwards battled back with several straight wins to lead the series by a single point before the final races at Imola. Fittingly, it is said the Imola track is built on the site of an ancient Roman chariot track. Bayliss, especially, arrived in San Marino in "win or crash" mode, since a win could mean the championship while even if he crashed, he could finish no lower than second overall. Edwards won the first race, which will go down in history as one of the closest and hardest fought races of all time. That meant that he could win the championship by safely staying behind Bayliss in the second race. He earned the respect of racing fans around the world by risking everything to win that race, too.

Day 131:
Lawson, Schwantz & Rainey – 1989 French Grand Prix

The 1989 season featured the most talent-laden 500cc grids of the two-stroke era. Wayne Rainey, Eddie Lawson and Kevin Schwantz were all at the height of their powers. Mick Doohan was an impressive rookie and even though Wayne Gardner was thinking of retiring, he could still win on his day. Randy Mamola was in the mix – perhaps the most talented rider who never won a world championship. Even Freddie Spencer made a comeback attempt that year.

The best race of the season took place at Le Mans, when Lawson, Schwantz and Rainey traded the lead an uncountable number of times before Lawson took the checkers.

Schwantz won the most races that year but Lawson once again proved that his "Steady Eddie" nickname was well-chosen. His consistency earned him his fourth and final world championship.

Day 132:
David Jefferies' fastest lap of the Isle of Man
After the death of Joey Dunlop in 2000, David Jefferies assumed the mantle of "greatest living TT rider." Where Dunlop had always *been* fast, he hadn't always *looked* fast since he rode with a very tidy and economical style. Jefferies was a different kettle of fish altogether. The big man put so much physical effort into riding that his mechanics had to replace his bikes' footpegs after each practice session – he bent them that badly! That made watching "DJ" memorable – and frightening. He set the outright lap record for the TT course during the 2002 Senior TT, at an average speed of 127.29 miles an hour. It was the last TT race he ever won. He was killed in practice the following spring.

Day 133:

Roger DeCoster – 1972 Australian Grand Prix

DeCoster, a Belgian, had been a fast but inconsistent rider in the late '60s. In 1971 he switched from CZ to Suzuki motorcycles and began a streak of incredibly dominant riding on a Suzuki RM370. He won the 500cc world championship in four of the next five seasons. That combination of man and machine proved its utter superiority at the 1972 Australian Grand Prix, when DeCoster lapped the entire field! Although specific "lapping" records are not kept, it may be the only time it happened in any form of world championship motocross.

Day 134:

Mike Duff's 120 mph lap of Spa

In 1964 Mike Duff, of Canada, became the first North American to win a motorcycle Grand Prix, when he won the 250cc Grand Prix of Belgium on the road circuit at Spa. Duff's fastest lap, at an average speed of over 120 mph, astounded the motorcycle press. With good reason: on a 250, it meant that he'd lapped almost the entire circuit absolutely wide open in top gear.

The greatest racers of the first 50 years

At the beginning of the 20th century, most European "road races" were held on unpaved roads. Here in the U.S., the Daytona 200 was held on the old beach course – half sand and half asphalt. That's why there's no point in distinguishing between "road" and "off-road" prowess among early riders. So who were the best of the best, back in the days when men were men and helmets were leather skull caps or, at best, a cork-lined "pudding bowl"?

Day 135:
Geoff Duke
In the early years of Grand Prix racing, Geoff Duke was universally recognized for his speed, smoothness and control. He won six Isle of Man TT races and was the 500cc world champion three times. An Englishman, he retired on the Isle of Man, scene of his greatest triumphs.

Day 136:
Stanley Woods
With a true Irishman's gift of the gab, Woods effectively charmed (some would say "conned") the Cotton motorcycle company into sponsoring his first efforts to win the TT. He may have been all talk at the beginning, but he was all action once he got a motorcycle – Woods won 10 TTs between 1923-'39.

Day 137:
Ed "Iron Man" Kretz
A great rider both before and after WWII, Kretz is best remembered for winning the first Daytona 200, in 1937. Although he never won the "200" again (due to a run of bad mechanical luck) he continued to race in it until he was 47. Kretz, who was from San Diego, was voted the most popular AMA racer in 1938 and again in '48 – more evidence of his durability. He won scores of races of all kinds and many of the stars of the '20s and '30s said he was the best racer they'd ever seen. His son was also a successful motorcycle racer.

Day 138:
Jimmy Guthrie
Guthrie, a Scot, learned to ride motorcycles as a dispatch rider in France in WWI. He was quiet and unassuming off his motorcycle but he was a fierce competitor on it. He won six TT races and many "classic" races on the continent in the 1930s. In 1935 alone he won the Swiss, Dutch, German, Belgian and Spanish Grands Prix. He also set many speed and endurance records. It's impossible to know how many races he might have won, as he was killed in the '37 German Grand Prix. Although he was already 40 and often the oldest man in the race, he had been a late bloomer and was still in his prime.

Day 139:
Joe Petrali

Petrali was from San Francisco but grew up in Sacramento, just a few blocks from the state fairgrounds where many motorcycle races were held. He became the greatest rider of 1920's and '30s, which was the heyday of AMA Class A racing. He won on board tracks, dirt tracks and even won many "endurance" races that, at the time, were competitions to see how far one could go on a gallon of gas. He had an advantage in such competitions because when he started out, he only weighted 80 pounds! In 1933, '34, '35 and '36, he was a national champ in both dirt track and hillclimb disciplines.

Day 140:
Joe Leonard

Leonard was another San Diegan. In '54, he won the first AMA Grand National Championship. (Until 1953, the AMA national championship was decided by a single winner-take-all race.) With nothing to compare it to, fans in that first season couldn't have appreciated Leonard's record of eight national wins in a single campaign (which would not happen until 1986) or his four-in-a-row streak (a record that stood until 1993.) He won the AMA GNC again in '56 and '57. An argument could easily be made that Leonard also deserves a spot on the "all-round" list; after quitting motorcycles, he came within a few laps of winning the Indy 500 auto race.

Day 141:
Carroll Resweber
A native of Port Arthur, Texas, Resweber won four consecutive Grand National Championships from 1958-'61. He won nationals on mile, half-mile and short track ovals, as well as a national championsip road race at Watkins Glen. He was one of the only riders capable of besting Joe Leonard in his prime and as impressive as his career was, there's no telling what he may have achieved had he not suffered a career-ending accident in 1962.

Day 142:
Lloyd "Sprouts" Elder
Elder began racing at the end of the board track era but rose to fame in Class A short track racing in the early '20s. Seeking greater challenges (and more prize money) he traveled to Australia to race during the American off-season. In 1927 he won the "golden helmet" Australian championship against stiff local competition as well as other top American and British riders.

Elder then traveled to Britain where he won a number of championships, including the prestigious Scottish "silver helmet." The magazine "Speedway News" rated him the most entertaining and popular rider of the day. He even raced in South America before finally resettling in California where he promoted speedway races. After retiring from racing, he joined the California Highway Patrol. Presumably, no speeders outran him.

Day 143:

Jacques "Jake" DeRosier

As his name implies, DeRosier was born in Quebec although he grew up in New England. As a young man in the late 1890's, he was a very successful bicycle racer. He saw some of the first motorized "pacers"– used to train bicycle racers. He soon became a skilled rider of the newfangled contraptions and took part exhibition races on them – those were the first motorcycle races in the U.S.

DeRosier's early wins came on small wooden velodromes. He also raced with great success on the larger motordrome board tracks that were built at the turn of the century. He traveled to England where he won many fans in a series of match races with the English champion Charlie Collier. He was a major star and one of the very first "factory" riders, racing professionally for Indian and Excelsior. By his own count he won 900 races, though it is not known if he included bicycle races in that tally. He suffered a serious crash in 1912 and died a long and painful year later, of medical complications.

Day 144:

Harold Daniell

Although he "only" won three TT races, Daniell is one of the few men to have won both before and after WWII. Had the war not intervened at the height of Daniell's powers, he would certainly have won many more. Ironically, at the very end of his career, he won the very first true world championship Grand Prix race. (There had been races called "Grand Prix" for years, but the FIM did not sanction a world championship series until '49.)

Daniell wore tiny round glasses and looked more like an insurance salesman than a motorcycle racer. When not racing, he worked as a development rider for Norton and he is now best remembered in that role. When the McCandless brothers built a new frame for Norton's Manx racer with a novel rear swingarm, they asked Daniell how if felt. He famously replied, "It's like a feather bed." For the next 20 years, "featherbed" Nortons dominated Grand Prix grids.

Masters of all trades and jacks of none

Most great motorcycle riders are specialists but a few have proven that they can master any two-wheeled discipline, or master both two and four wheels. So who are the most versatile riders?

Day 145:
John Surtees

Only one man has ever won the top class in the motorcycle road racing world championship and the Formula One automobile championship. John Surtees, an Englishman, won seven motorcycle world titles in the 1950s. His 500cc Grand Prix championships came in '56 and '58 through '60 on MV Agusta motorcycles.

In 1960 he raced both motorcycles and cars, initially for Lotus. In 1964 he switched to Ferrari, winning the championship the same year. Later on, he formed his own F-1 team.

Day 146:
Dick "Bugsy" Mann

Mann was the AMA Grand National Champion twice in the years when GNC points were awarded for both dirt track and road races. He is one of the few riders who've won AMA championship races on paved tracks as well as mile, half-mile, short-track and TT style dirt tracks. As impressive as that is, it doesn't begin to cover the full range of his talents. Mann also was a very competitive rider in national-championship motocross when that sport was in its U.S. infancy.

He also had the longest career of any top AMA rider, finishing in the top 10 in the AMA GNC every year but one from 1957-'73. He retired from professional competition in 1974 and, incredibly, qualified for and competed in the 1975 ISDT, winning a bronze medal.

Day 147:
Jean-Michel Bayle

Bayle, a Frenchman, won the World Motocross titles in the 125cc class in 1988 and the 250cc class in '89. Most of the European tracks he raced on were fast and relatively smooth, so no one expected him to win the U.S. Supercross title in '91. He also won the U.S. outdoor championships that year in both the 250cc and 500cc classes.

Bayle had insisted that his contract with Honda include a chance to test a road racing motorcycle. On a testing trip to Japan, Honda offered him a ride on an NSR250 road racer. Even though he'd only ridden street bikes a few times, he lapped the test track within a second of another Honda test rider, who was a Japanese road racing champion.

After making the switch to road racing full time, Bayle finished a credible 8th in the 250cc world championship. In 1996, he was ranked 9th in the premier 500cc class. Although he never won as a top-level Grand Prix racer, he proved that he deserved his ride by qualifying on the front row. His road racing career was cut short by a series of serious concussions. Not surprisingly, he was also a world-class supermoto rider. He was once overheard saying, "If I win the 500cc world championship, I'll switch to trials riding."

Day 148:
Jeff Ward
From the mid-1980s to the early '90s, "Wardy" won no less than seven national motocross titles. He than moved to open wheel race-cars first in the Indy Lights class and later in the IRL. In 1999, he finished second in the Indianapolis 500. After retiring from that, he came back to motorcycles and was one of the leading riders in the brief heyday of the AMA Supermoto championships.

Day 149:
Sammy Miller
Road racing and motorcycle trials have, it would seem, almost nothing in common. Sammy Miller is famous as one of the greatest trials riders of all time. He won well over 1,000 trials, and played a key role in the development of three generations of trials motorcycles, for Ariel, then Bultaco, and finally Honda. Nowadays, many people forget that he was also a world-class road racer

He was Irish, so not surprisingly he came to the fore at road races like the Cookstown 100, which he won several times. He also had several top-10 finishes on the Isle of Man. Miller finished second in the 1957 250cc world championship aboard a Mondial, before he gave up road racing to focus on trials, which was much more popular then than it is today.

Day 150:
Mike Hailwood
Hailwood established himself as the greatest motorcycle racer of all time the 1960s. With nothing left to prove on two wheels, he set out to become the Formula One car champ.

He won the European Formula Two championship in '72, driving for John Surtees' team. The next year he switched to McLaren and again showed good speed but crashed heavily at the Nurburgring, ending a promising car-racing career.

In 1978, Hailwood announced a return to the Isle of Man TT races, where he'd won his greatest victories. Between the late '60s and the late '70s, road racing had changed dramatically. Thanks to improvements in tires and suspension, cornering speeds were much higher. Racers now all hung off and put their knees down – a technique that was faster but far more physically tiring than the classic, tucked in style from Hailwood's championship years. Mike the Bike proved his doubters wrong when he won the 1978 TT on a Ducati. Ironically the class he won was, also, called Formula One.

Day 151:
Alberto "Johnny" Cecotto
This Venezuelan won the 1975 350cc world championship. He won the '76 Daytona 200. In '78, he finished third overall in the 500cc GP title chase and won the 750cc F-1 championship. However, a series of late-'70s crashes eroded his abilities on two wheels and he decided to try four.

In 1982, he came within a hair's breadth of winning the European Formula Two championship, tying his BMW-March team-mate but finishing second based on the number of wins. Still, it was enough to warrant offers in Formula One.

His run of bad luck with injuries continued. In '84, he crashed his F-1 Toleman car while practicing for the British Grand Prix and broke both his legs. That crash ended his F-1 career and he watched while his Toleman team-mate, Ayrton Senna, went on to glory. Even so, Cecotto had a productive career in the '90s in European touring car racing, twice winning the hotly-contest German championship.

Day 152:
Hubert Auriol and Stephane Peterhansel
Since it's creation in 1979, the epic "Paris-Dakar" off-road race has often been called the world's most difficult motor race. Two men, both French, have succeeded in winning it on both two wheels and four wheels. Hubert Auriol did it first. He won on bikes in '81 and '83. He broke both his ankles on the penultimate day of the '87 rally and switched to cars in '88. He won on four wheels in '92. Not to be outdone, Stephane Peterhansel won the Paris-Dakar an incredible five times on bikes in the 1990s, then won in a car in 2004.

Day 153:

Malcolm Smith

Smith is best known for his role in On Any Sunday
and his desert-racing exploits. He was, however, an
astonishingly versatile rider. In one memorable scene
from the film, he arrives at a national championship
hillclimb event, having never even seen one before.
All the other riders have specialized hillclimb bikes
but Smith arrives with a trials bike. On his first
attempt, he nearly wins the event. He was often asked
to race in national or international championships but
always refused, saying he liked to stay within a day's
drive of his home, so he could always get back to his
business on Monday morning.

Cunning stunts: don't try these at home

As if riding motorcycles – or racing them – wasn't dangerous enough, there have always been thrill-seekers who've risked their lives to perform the longest jump or fastest wheelie. "What?" you ask, "the Starboyz didn't invent riding like lunatics?" Oh no, dear reader, those pups are mere upstarts compared to these godfathers of oh-my-God.

Day 154:
Evel Knievel
No motorcyclist has ever had as big an impact on American popular culture as Robert Craig "Evel" Knievel. In the early 1970s he was the only motorcyclist that the average American could identify but saying that doesn't do justice to his fame – he was one of the most recognizable celebrities on the planet.

Knievel rose to that fame by accident – literally. In '68, he planned to jump a motorcycle over the fountains at Caesar's Palace in Las Vegas. He pitched the stunt to television networks and none of them wanted to broadcast it. However, ABC told him that if he filmed the jump himself, they'd look at it afterwards.

Knievel arranged for a film-maker named John Derek to document the jump. (Derek was briefly famous himself as the discoverer-publicist- husband of '70s sex-symbol Bo Derek.) Knievel's jump was great but the landing was a disaster. The spectacular crash was featured on ABC's Wide World of Sports. Knievel emerged from a coma to find that he'd become a star.

Day 155:
Bud Ekins
Knievel's monster wipeout may have been the most-watched jump on television but the most-watched jump in the *movies* was a stunt in the 1963 film The Great Escape. Although the film's star Steve McQueen was a skilled and aggressive motorcycle rider, the producers wouldn't allow him to perform his own stunts, so that jump was made by McQueen's friend and racing mentor Bud Ekins.

Ekins was a veteran Hollywood stunt man and one of the top desert racers in southern California. Although in the story, McQueen's character has stolen a German military-issue motorcycle, the stunt was performed on one of Ekins' Triumph desert racing bikes, repainted in drab military colors.

Day 156:
Seth Enslow
Hundreds of straight-to-video productions followed the first groundbreaking (and bone-breaking) Crusty Demons of Dirt. The highlight was Seth Enslow's nearly 100-yard dune jump. This eye-popping stunt was made without the benefit of a takeoff ramp, landing ramp, foresight or, indeed, any instinct for self-preservation at all.

Day 157:
Louis "Speedy" Babbs

After a poor childhood in Kentucky and a few years working in the coal mines, Babbs moved to southern California in the 1920s. He was one of the first Hollywood stunt men and often did motorcycle stunts. In 1929, he began performing a "wall of death" act on the permanent midway at Venice Beach. This involved riding his motorcycle on the vertical walls of large wooden cylinder.

Babbs was not the first wall of death rider but he was certainly the hardest working man in that (admittedly obscure) branch of show business. After more than 20 years touring with his "drome" as he called it, he created a spherical, steel-framed "globe of death" in which he performed even more hair-raising stunts. He kept it up well into his sixties. He was a natural showman who, when asked if he feared being killed during his act once quipped, "Do you plan on leaving this earth alive?"

Day 158:
Travis Pastrana

Pastrana was a world champ in the fledgling sport of FMX at the age of 14. He once went six years without being beaten in freestyle competition. He was one of the first people to perform a motorcycle backflip and the first to perfect a "360" mid-air spin. He hails from Annapolis, MD. That's an appropriate address since in his line of "work" he spends a lot of time at the M.D. By his own count he's endured 19 surgeries – on his knees alone. Other injuries include countless concussions and a broken back.

Day 159:
Mike Metzger
Metzger is Pastrana's west-coast nemesis. He's certainly able to match Travis' medical horror stories, boasting no less than three broken backs and numerous arm and leg fractures, including both femurs. This X-Games gold medalist was the first person to successfully land a "ramp-to-dirt" backflip.

Mike revisited the site of Evel Knievel's most famous motorcycle stunt. He did a backflip while clearing the fountains at Caesar's Palace. The 125-foot jump was the longest backflip ever.

Day 160:
Rollie Free
The aptly named Free was a motorcycle racer as a young man but is remembered mainly as the subject of the most famous motorcycle photo ever. The picture shows Free, laying flat on a Vincent Black Shadow, wearing nothing but a bathing suit, on the Bonneville Salt Flats.

Free had set several speed records at Daytona Beach before going to the Salt Flats in 1948. That year, he set a record at 148 miles per hour but wanted to reach 150. Thinking that his leather suit was causing drag, Free stripped and put on a skimpy bathing suit. Lying horizontally on the Vincent's fuel tank, stretched out like Superman, he did in fact go 150. Although Free was the guy who earned eternal fame for the stunt, he later admitted that he got the idea after watching Ed Kretz do the same thing at a speed trial on a California dry lake.

In 1950, Free returned to the salt and pushed his record to 156. He survived a high-speed crash that Speed Week – thankfully while wearing full leathers!

Day 161:
Special shared award: McCrary Twins
Billy and Benny McCrary were born in Hendersonville NC in 1946. Although they were small babies (just over 5 pounds) they quickly grew to become the world's heaviest twins, weighing in at well over 700 pounds each. Although they are now usually remembered as pro wrestlers they were also known for the motorcycle stunts they performed on Honda SL100 minibikes. To be honest, I don't know what "stunts" they could possibly have done, but who cares? Just riding at all must have stunned onlookers. One imagines them getting ready to do their act…

Billy: "I can't find my bike."
Benny: "You're sitting on it."
In the '70s they rode the tiny bikes across the U.S., traveling 3000 miles and amply proving the ruggedness of Honda's products. In 1979, Billy suffered what should have been a minor injury during their stunt act and died of heart failure. Touchingly, his brother buried him back in Hendersonville, under the world's largest granite tombstone. Benny died of heart failure at 54, and he too was buried under the stone, which is decorated with images of their beloved minibikes.

Day 162:

Special shared award #2: Anonymous nutcases on the 'net

What makes America great? The widespread availability of powerful motorcycles. Lots of small, high-quality digital video cameras. And last but not least, a ready supply of young men who know that anything their mothers told them not to do must be really fun.

The best thing about this combination (already enough to strike terror into health care insurance providers) is that people seem especially willing to share their home videos when things go horribly wrong. In fact there are web sites devoted to nothing but such foolishness. Just Google the phrase 'motorcycle fail' and amuse yourself for hours.

Things even "HOG" members don't know about Harley-Davidson

Harley-Davidson is the oldest continuously operated motorcycle company in the world. In its 100+ years, "The Motor Company" has obviously written a large share of the history of the motorcycle. There's lots for the company to be proud of, and a few moments that probably make Harley historians wince. Once, when I was at the company's official museum, a curator told me that Arthur Davidson fit perfectly into his wife's clothes. In fact, he wore her clothes to parties, where he sat on men's laps, flirted, and kissed them on the cheek.

"Times were different back then," the museum guy chuckled. "Can you imagine a modern industrialist doing that?" Actually, what I can't imagine is Harley-Davidson's customers wrapping their heads around it. Suffice it to say that, while the museum has a room devoted to all of the different Harley motors, I don't expect a room devoted to the Davidson trannies any time soon.

Day 163:
Improving the bicycle. And the rowboat
In 1901, William S. Harley and Arthur Davidson began working on a 116cc auxiliary motor for a bicycle. That motor was never able to power a bicycle up Milwaukee's hills. A couple of years later, the pair were joined by Walter Davidson. They made a much more powerful 405cc motor with the assistance of Ole Evinrude – better known as the inventor of the outboard motor.

Day 164:
Belts go in and out of fashion
Harleys were among the last motorcycles to abandon leather belts for chain drives, around 1914. Leather belts slipped, stretched and rotted, so chains were a big improvement. But modern belts provide a smoother ride than chains, last longer, and free riders from the drudgery of chain lubrication and adjustment. Harley was the first company to go back to all-belt drive (except for a couple of limited-production race bikes) in 1992.

Day 165:
When a Harley "hog" was a real pig
In the 1920s, the official Harley-Davidson factory racing team was so dominant that it was nicknamed the "wrecking crew." The crew's mascot was a small pig. Eventually, the bikes came to be known as hogs. In 1999, the company failed in an attempt to trademark "hog" when the United States Court of Appeals for the Second Circuit ruled that the term applied to all heavyweight cruisers (and actual pigs.)

Day 166:

Harley does BMW

When U.S. soldiers captured their first "Wehrmacht"-issue motorcycles in World War II, they found that those BMWs and Zundapps were better suited to tough military duty. Harley-Davidson and Indian each developed about 1,000 machines for evaluation, with shaft drives and flat-twin motors copied from the Germans. They were never widely issued, though the machines cost Uncle Sam a whopping $35,000 each.

Day 167:

Think the first Harley with an electric starter was the Electra-Glide? Think again

That honor goes to the humble three-wheeled Servi-Car delivery vehicle – it got an electric starter in 1964, a year before the introduction of Electra-Glide.

Day 168:

The XR750's debut was inauspicious, to say the least

Through most of the 1960s, Harley-Davidson influenced the AMA to give the side-valve Harley race bikes a 250cc displacement advantage. In 1968, the AMA changed Class C racing rules to allow both foreign and domestic makers to race 750cc bikes. Harley knew it had to build a new race bike, so it created the XR750. The bike made its first appearance at Daytona in 1970. Cal Rayborn was Harley's star rider, but his XR didn't last the race. In fact, none of the factory XRs managed to run the whole 200 miles. The first Harley across the line was an ancient KR model, first introduced in 1952. The rider was Walt Fulton III.

Day 169:
Harley riders don't hang out in cafes, they hang out in bars
Although most Harley fans would rather forget the years in which the company was owned by AMF, there is one AMF-era bike that's highly sought-after by collectors: the 1977 XLCR. That "CR" stands for Café Racer and the bike was only the second major project for Willie G. Davidson (the grandson of one of the founders.) While the model is prized now, it was rejected by Harley customers in 1977. Only 3,100 were sold and the model was dropped a year later – although dealers still had unsold XLCRs cluttering their showroom floors well into the '80s.

Day 170:
The first Buell motorcycle was a two-stroke
Erik Buell started his company to build affordable production racers. He invested his life's savings to prototype the RW750 (the initials stood for "Road Warrior"). It was powered by a 750cc square-four two-stroke motor. Just as Buell was about to begin production, the AMA changed the rules. With the stroke of a pen, they made his inventory and tooling obsolete. Buell then decided to try and fit a tuned Sportster motor in his lightweight, sporty chassis. The rest is history.

Day 171:

Want the rarest modern Harley? Head for Poland...

When Harley-Davidson decided to build the VR1000 superbike, race rules specified that the company had to also build and sell 2,000 machines for road use. This process is called "homologation". So, you may wonder, why have you never seen a road-going VR1000 if 2000 were sold? Because the model was homologated in Poland. By selling it there, Harley avoided U.S. liability and Poland's lax laws allowed the barely-modified race bike to be legally licensed.

Day 172:

That's "potato potato," not "potato™ potato™"

Despite spending tens of thousands of dollars in legal fees in the mid-'90s – and having initial success in its efforts to trademark the sound of Harley motors – the company dropped its U.S. Patent Office application in 2000.

Harley-Davidson's vice president of marketing, Joanne Bischmann, told reporters, "I've personally spoken with Harley-Davidson owners from around the world and they've told me repeatedly that there is nothing like the sound of a Harley-Davidson motorcycle. If our customers know the sound cannot be imitated, that's good enough for me and for Harley-Davidson."

Harley History – 10 hogs that matter

Are you the sort of person who lies awake at night imagining the "dream garage" of vintage Harleys you'd collect after winning the Powerball lottery? If so, here's list to get you started – historically significant hogs from each decade in the 20th century.

Day 173:
1900-'09 – the first "Silent Gray Fellow"
Most of the first decade's Harley-Davidsons had single-cylinder motors. Although production began in 1903, only a handful of bikes were made prior to '06 when the displacement increased from 24.7 to 26.8 cu. in., boosting output to 4 horsepower. That year Harley-Davidson began painting their motorcycles gray, instead of black. Thanks to their well-designed mufflers (at a time when many motorcycles ran open headers) they earned the nickname "Silent Gray Fellows." The name evoked solid reliability and was used for decades.

Day 174:
1910-'19 – Model 7D
Bill Harley had experimented with a V-twin motor in 1907 and the company sold its first twins in '09, but they were not ready for prime time. The 1911 Model

7D was a fine machine, however. It had a 49 cu. in. motor that produced about 6 horsepower. Its only weakness was its leather drive belt. Harley finally adopted chain drives for all models in 1913.

Day 175:
1920-'29 – Twin-cam JDH
In 1922, Harley's first 74 cu. in. motors appeared on the JD and FD models. In 1928, these bikes got high-performance twin-cam motors that gave them top speeds of nearly 100 miles an hour.

Day 176:
1930-'39 – Knucklehead
The first EL model, with an overhead valve 61 cu. in. motor, appeared in 1936. Because of the shape of its rocker boxes, it quickly came to be called the "knucklehead." The motor was used until '47 and became the ultimate chopper motor. Custom builders still favor them.

Day 177:
1940-'49 – Hydra-Glide
In 1948, Harley's workhorse 61 and 74 cu. in. motors got a much needed update, with aluminum heads and hydraulic valve lifters. The new heads had chromed valve covers shaped like cake pans, hence the name Panhead. The following year, the Hydra-Glide was the first (non-military) Harley-Davidson model supplied with an up-to-date hydraulic front fork.

Day 178:
1950-'59 – Sportster
Through the '50s, America's sporting riders became more and more attracted to lighter and more agile British 650s. In the first part of the decade Harley-Davidson built the K motor, which was more compact, thanks to unit construction (the crankcase and transmission were cast together.) But that was not enough to compete with BSAs and Triumphs on performance.

In 1957, the company responded by putting overhead valves on the K motor, to create the 55 cu. in. Sportster. It was the last mass produced Harley-Davidson sport bike until the introduction of XR1200x about 50 years later.

Day 179:
1960-'69 – Electra-Glide
The first Harley with rear suspension was the Duo-Glide, introduced in '58. In 1965, the Duo-Glide got an electric starter and a new name, Electra-Glide.

Day 180:
1970-'79 – XR750 Production Racer
Most Harley lovers would rather forget the years in which the company was owned by AMF. But AMF didn't prevent the introduction of the company's most beautiful bike: the XR750 production racer. The first XRs appeared in 1970 but they were beset with problems. In '72, the XR got new aluminum heads and Mark Brelsford immediately won the AMA Grand National Championship.

Day 181:
1980-'89 – Softail

A group of Harley managers bought the company in '81, ending the dark years under AMF. In 1984, the company introduced the all-new 1340cc Evolution motor. It was cooler, quieter and vastly more reliable than anything seen before. The "Evo" motor was used in several new models, notably the Softail which concealed the rear suspension allowing stylists to evoke Harley's long heritage. The combination of new and old in the same bike struck a chord with buyers, who flocked back to company.

Day 182:
1990-'99 – VR1000

In this decade, most new Harleys were essentially styling exercises. There was one absolute break with tradition, however. It was the VR1000 superbike that Harley raced in the AMA Superbike Championship. The best thing one could say about the VR1000 was that it was at least as fast as its principal rivals... had been a couple of years earlier.

In order to race the VR1000, Harley also had to homologate (ie, sell) a similar street bike. Curiously, AMA rules didn't require it to be sold here. To limit liability and pollution control costs, the street legal VR1000s were sold in Poland. Yes, Poland. American collectors were allowed to re-import them as long as they promised never to use them on public roads.

Nowadays, revisionist historians at The Motor Company like to pretend that the VR1000 had been a development project intended only to pave the way for the V-Rod. That's a load of hooey. Harley wanted to win superbike races and was bitterly disappointed that it never could.

That said, the VR1000 street bike was basically a factory superbike with lights, mirrors, and a starter motor. It was by far the best-performing Harley street bike ever made. It's not surprising the entire fifty-bike production run was snapped up by collectors in spite of the $50,000 price tag.

Honda History – the ultimate 10-Honda collection

No company has had a greater impact on the modern motorcycle than Honda. It rose from the humblest of beginnings in postwar Japan to become the world's largest motorcycle manufacturer – a status it had by 1960, before most Americans had even heard of it! Since then it has become one of the world's most advanced car companies, a major manufacturer of jet engines and a global leader in robotics, all without losing sight of its origins.

It's easy to fantasize about a Honda collection that includes the factory Grand Prix race bikes but in recent years the company has flatly refused to sell them at any price. If you want one, there's only one way to get it: become a Honda factory rider and win a world championship on one of its bikes. Then, the company will give you one.

Since that's out of reach, even for early employees of Microsoft, this is a list of production bikes.

Day 183:
Model D
The first Hondas were war-surplus generator motors converted for use on bicycles. When the initial supply of surplus motors ran out, Honda started making its own. Its first real motorcycle was the 98cc Model D made in 1948-'49. When the first prototype was shown to the twenty employees in the Honda factory, one of them shouted, "It's like a dream!" The name Dream was used for many subsequent Honda models.

Day 184:
NR750
In 1979, Honda made an abortive attempt to build a four-stroke 500GP motorcycle that could compete with the two-strokes. The NR500 was one of the company's rare failures although it proved that the unique "oval piston" technology was viable. It was not until 1992 that oval pistons briefly appeared in a production motorcycle – the NR750.

The NR750 was Honda's "ultimate motorcycle" and the incredible motor (nominally a V-four but with 8 con rods, 8 spark plugs, and 32 valves) was only part of its over-the-top specification. It also had electronic fuel injection, a single-sided swingarm, carbon-fiber bodywork, magnesium wheels – and a $60,000 price tag. About 200 were made.

Day 185:
Model E
Until the introduction of the model E in 1951, virtually all Japanese motorcycles (including Hondas) were two-strokes. They made crowded Japanese streets noisy, smoky and altogether unpleasant. Soichiro Honda grew to hate them.

By comparison, Honda's first four-stroke, the Model E, was quite civilized. Honda wasn't the only one pleased by the improvement. Within a couple of years Japanese motorcyclists were buying them by the tens of thousands. Profit from the Model E funded a huge research and development effort that led to many more advanced machines.

Day 186:
CB750
Honda introduced the CB750 at the end of 1968 but it didn't hit the market until early '69. Until well into 1970, CB750s were made with sand-cast, not die-cast engine cases. In truth, die-cast cases were lighter, stronger, and more oil tight. But it's the sand-cast models that are prized by collectors.

Day 187:
RC30
The RC30 was introduced in 1987. It was essentially a street-legal version of Honda's factory endurance racer. It was by far the most sophisticated – and in many peoples' opinion, the most beautiful – sport bike of its time.

Day 188:
CB92 "Benly"
In the early '60s, Honda was already fielding very competitive Grand Prix racers, even though the company's street bikes were still all simple, utilitarian transport. The introduction of the 125cc Benly changed that. The pressed-steel frame took its cues from the small German sport bikes of the period, like the NSU Sportmax. The twin-cylinder motor however, was based on Honda's own R&D. It spun to 10,500 rpm.

Day 189:
CR250 "Elsinore"
In the early '70s, Honda finally admitted that in order to build a competitive 250cc motocrosser, the company would have to make a two-stroke motor – even though Mr. Honda himself reviled such motors. The 1973 CR250 was immediately the most effective production race bike in its class, and Gary Jones won the AMA motocross championship on it in its first year.

Day 190:
CB1100F
The CB750 motor continued to evolve, getting dual overhead cams and a displacement increase to over 900cc. Its highest expression came in the RCB factory endurance racers, which inspired the CB900F "Bol d'Or" street bike. That bike was sold in the U.S. in the early '80s. Finally, in 1983, the CB1100F brought this noble line of machines to its conclusion. It was the best air-cooled superbike ever made.

Day 191:
GL 1000 Gold Wing
This iconic touring motorcycle hit the market in '75. Although the water-cooled four-cylinder "boxer" engine layout had been proven in cars, it was quite shocking to see it in a motorcycle. The motor proved to be smooth and very powerful. The 'Wing was heavy, but Honda kept its center of gravity low by storing the fuel under the seat, so the handling was surprisingly good.

Day 192:
CBX
When it was introduced in 1979 the stunning-looking six-cylinder CBX was the quickest production motorcycle ever tested on the dragstrip. Nowadays, the CBX has a cult of obsessive collector-fans.

To tell the truth, the CBX never had the chassis it needed to match that motor. It was sold for two years as a sports bike but it didn't really handle that well. For another couple of years it was fashioned as a sort of "power tourer" and sold with a fairing and saddlebags. Don't tell members of the cult, but that version didn't sell too well either and Honda retired the model after a short, four-year life. That kept total production numbers low which makes them even rarer today.

It seemed like a good idea at the time

The modern motorcycle is a machine, not an animal, so there's no evolution vs. intelligent design debate. However, looking back at the bikes on this list, you might want to debate intelligent design vs. plain stupid design.

This list includes a handful of bikes that were before their time, another handful of terrible ideas whose time would never have come in a million years, and one very strange motorcycle that has been on the market almost unchanged for half a century.

Day 193:
Roadog
"Wild Bill" Gelbke was an aeronautical engineer who worked for McDonnell-Douglas, before packing it in during the '60s to pursue his dream of building an advanced, shaft-drive motorcycle equipped with disc brakes, twin headlights, and an automatic transmission.

Some dream. Gelbke's bike (he dubbed it "Roadog") was more like a nightmare. It was powered by a four-cylinder 152 cu. in. Chevy motor and the shaft drive mechanism incorporated the differential from a pickup truck. It weighed over *three thousand* pounds.

According to legend, no one but Gelbke could ride the beast. Still, ride it he did – thousands of miles on a whim, just to go for a steak or a beer. Gelbke built a second Roadog for a friend.

They say there's a fine line between genius and madness and no one who has ever seen the Roadog disputes it. "Wild Bill" Gelbke was killed in the late '70s in a shootout with police when a domestic dispute took a turn for the worst. The Roadog didn't turn well, either.

Day 194:
Bimota V-due
Although this Italian firm was chronically underfinanced, it built a great reputation in the '70s and '80s by buying other companies' motors and installing them in beautiful, sweet-handling chassis of its own design.

The V-due was announced in the mid-'90s. It was to be a fire-breathing 500cc Grand Prix bike for the street. With a projected power output of about 110 hp and a weight of just 360 pounds, the V-due promised the best power-to-weight ratio of any production motorcycle. The first year's run was completely pre-sold.

The biggest technical challenge Bimota faced was making a 500cc two-stroke motor that could meet emissions control rules for road use. The company conceived an ingenious direct-injection system in which a stream of liquid fuel was sprayed onto the piston crown where it immediately evaporated. On paper, it produced an efficient air-fuel mixture and helped to cool the motor, too.

There was only one problem: the V-due wasn't ridden on paper, it was ridden on asphalt. In 1998 the first customers took possession of their V-dues and quickly realized that the fuel-injection system was entirely unworkable. Bimota recalled the machines and went bankrupt trying to figure out a way to make them actually work.

Day 195:
Yamaha GTS 1000
In the early '90s, Yamaha placed a huge emphasis on the GTS1000 in an attempt convince motorcyclists that it, not Honda, built the world's most sophisticated bikes. It hired the iconoclastic motorcycle designer James Parker to create a single-sided front swingarm with hub-center steering.

The unique front suspension was only the most visible of the GTS' many innovations, which included ABS and fuel injection. The company knew that if it released this technological *tour de force* as a pure sport bike, motorcycle magazines would determine success or failure on the basis of comparative performance alone. So, they built the GTS as a sports-tourer.

The GTS1000 was a great bike that handled brilliantly (despite weighing well over 600 pounds and being a handful at slow speed.) However, customers proved to be more traditional than designers. Whether due to its odd looks or $13,000 price tag (about $3,000 more than rival sports-tourers) it languished on dealers' floors. The bike was sold only in 1993-'94, then Yamaha pulled it off the market in frustration.

Day 196:
Honda 750A

The 18th Century lexicographer and blowhard Samuel Johnson once said, "Sir, a woman preaching is like a dog's walking on his hind legs. It is not done well; but you are surprised to find it done at all." That was more or less how motorcycle magazines reacted to the "Hondamatic" transmission when it was introduced in 1976. It worked, but sapped power and added 30 pounds to a motorcycle that was already a bit too heavy.

Although Honda's marketing department thought the automatic tranny would attract many new buyers, it didn't. Like the magazine's critics, consumers were underwhelmed and the 750A was quietly withdrawn in '78.

Day 197:
Munch Mammoth

In the mid-'60s, Friedl Munch designed a motorcycle powered by a 1,000cc NSU car motor (later Mammoths had 1,200cc and finally 1,300cc mills.)

Although it was visually massive, Munch's creation was no heavier than a Honda 750 and it was a scream to ride. Munch claimed it was geared to cruise at 140 miles an hour, although it had wide handlebars and no fairing, so only riders with necks as thick as an elephant's could actually know.

Floyd Clymer briefly imported the Mammoth into the U.S. Unfortunately, they were three times the price of a Honda 750 and customers waited so long to get them that it seemed they were delivered by glacier. Amazingly, Mammoths never actually went extinct. Munch supervised the manufacturing of a few bikes a year into the '90s.

Day 198:
Suzuki RE5
In many ways, the German engineer Felix Wankel's literally revolutionary motor was well suited to motorcycles. It generated a lot of power but was small, light and vibration-free. In the early '70s Suzuki licensed Wankel's design. The RE5 was to be Suzuki's flagship and the company spent millions building an entirely new production line for it.

Legend has it that the engine life was so short and rebuilding it was so difficult that Suzuki shipped a spare motor for every cycle, so it could simply be swapped out. Although that was almost certainly an exaggeration, customers avoided the RE5. Frustrated, Suzuki restyled it in an effort to make it look more conventional. The last year of production was 1976 but dealers had so much stock that many were sold as new '77s. According to another story, Suzuki managers took all the tooling for the bike out to sea and sunk it, so they would not be reminded of their decision to produce it.

Day 199:
Roberts KR3
Kenny Roberts was an AMA Grand National Champion, then the 500cc Grand Prix champion, and even won world championships as the manager of Yamaha's factory team. In 1996, he set out to prove that by using talent largely drawn from the pool of Formula One car engineers, he could build a winning

Grand Prix motorcycle from scratch.

Roberts spent millions building a state-of-the-art R&D facility in Banbury, England. His ex-F1 engineers determined a V-3 motor was optimal even though all the top 500GP teams used V-4s. He was not shy about saying he'd soon put his Japanese rivals including Yamaha (bikes he'd ridden to all his own championships) and Honda (a company he *hated*) in their place.

Roberts consistently fielded beautifully presented machines, but no KR3 rider ever finished the season in the top 10.

Day 200:
BMW C1
In 1992, BMW introduced the C1, a scooter with a roof. The rider sat in a car-like chair complete with a four-point seatbelt harness. BMW thought commuters in clogged European cities wanted the safety of a car and the parking ease and traffic filtering ability of a motorcycle. The company lobbied governments to allow C1 riders to operate it without a helmet. Britain, an essential market, refused. In any case, operating a C1 required a motorcycle license. The people who had such licenses – motorcyclists – never took to the bulbous C1, and car drivers couldn't be bothered to get a special license for it. BMW abandoned the concept in 2002.

Day 201:
BSA Ariel-3

By 1970, BSA's days were numbered and management was getting desperate. That year, the company launched a 50cc three-wheeled moped. The front wheel of the moped leaned into turns in the conventional manner but both rear wheels stayed in contact with the ground since the frame was hinged in the middle. The Ariel-3 handled about as well as you probably expect and the British motorcycle press thought it was ludicrous. Production ceased in '71. BSA did license some of the patents involved however. Honda produced two conceptually similar vehicles, the Stream and Giro. Neither of them were commercially viable, either.

Day 202:
Rokon "Mototractor"

About 50 years ago, a California inventor cobbled together the first (and so far, almost the only) two-wheel drive motorcycle. The Rokon company was created to manufacture it, with an initial investment from the founder of Merle Norman cosmetics. It's still in business and its product has hardly evolved.

Since a chain drive to the front wheel makes suspension impossible, the ride is cushioned only by the low-pressure tractor-style tires. This is not much of a problem, as the machine is intended for use at walking speeds. Curiously, although it is equipped with a three-speed transmission, Rokon recommends riders *stop* to change gears.

Motorcyclists have always rejected Rokons. In an *"I wouldn't be caught dead in any club that would accept me as a member"* reaction, Rokon does not call its product a motorcycle at all, but refers to it as a mototractor. Most Rokon models sell for about $5,000. For information on the only motorcycle that floats, visit www.rokonron.com or call 603-335 3200.

Gone but not forgotten – Great American motorcycles from the past

Between the turn of the century and the stock market crash of '29, as many as 200 American motorcycle companies were formed, produced and sold machines, then went bankrupt.

These companies didn't fail because their bikes weren't good, or because they couldn't compete with other motorcycle manufacturers. For the most part they failed because they were unable to sell their bikes at prices that could compete with Ford's Model T car.

It's interesting to wonder what the American motorcycle business would look like today if more of them had survived. Would domestic competition have forced Harley-Davidson and Indian to adopt newer technology? Would Indian have survived as a result? Would Harleys now be as technically advanced as BMWs? No one will ever know. What's certain however is that these American motorcycle companies were the state of the art in their day.

Day 203:

Crocker

Albert Crocker had been the West coast Indian distributor before he decided to build his own motorcycles. At first he build speedway racers but between 1936 and '41, he produced about 75 V-twin street bikes with displacements from 60-90 cu. in. They were the superbikes of their day, with overhead valve motors far more sophisticated than anything Harley or Indian put on the road. Some went 110 miles an hour. Crocker's small Los Angeles workshop never permitted him to produce enough machines to supply a dealer network.

Day 204:

Henderson

The Henderson motorcycle company was founded by Bill Henderson in 1911 and quickly became known for its four-cylinder models. Over the next few years, displacements increased from 1068cc to 1301cc. The bikes produced about 7 horsepower, which was considered a lot. More importantly, they started easily, ran smoothly, and didn't leak oil.

Henderson's fours were so good that Ignatz Schwinn licensed the design for his Excelsior company in 1917. Henderson continued producing a similar four-cylinder motorcycle he called the "ACE." He was killed in a motorcycle accident in 1922 and although the Henderson company hired another respected motorcycle designer, Arthur Lemon, to take his place, the company closed its doors in 1931.

Day 205:

Neracar

Pronounced "near a car," the name of this motorcycle was actually based on the name of the designer – J. Neracher. He began producing motorcycles in 1921. His designs were strikingly original, with hub-center steering and a very long, low layout in which the rider sat, car-style, in a chair behind the engine.

Most were powered by simple two-stroke motors but their low profile and streamlined, fully enclosed bodywork made them surprisingly fast. "Cannonball" Baker used a Neracar to set a transcontinental record. That was not enough publicity to prevent the company folding in 1926.

Day 206:

Pierce

The George N. Pierce company made bird cages and bathtubs before it produced the famed Pierce Arrow cars. Beginning in 1909, George's son Percy ran a subsidiary business making bicycles and motorcycles. Like the cars, Pierce motorcycles were top quality and commanded a top dollar – a shaft-drive, four-cylinder Pierce sold for $400. Motorcycle production lasted just four years, although the company continued making cars until 1936.

Day 207:

Yale

California Motor Company began making motorcycles in San Francisco as early as 1901. In 1903, George Wyman became the first person to ride across the country, a feat that clearly proved the

California's technical merit and durability. The tooling and manufacturing rights to that machine were sold to the Consolidated Manufacturing Co. in Toledo, OH. Yale-California motorcycles (later known simply as Yale) were sold from 1903-1913.

Day 208:
Flying Merkel
The historical record is murky concerning the origins of the Flying Merkel, which certainly had the catchiest name among all American brands. Joseph Merkel first manufactured motorcycles in Milwaukee in 1902. His motors used ball-bearings in place of bushings and he was one of the first makers to use cams to open inlet valves.

Merkel's company was bought and sold several times, moving to Pottstown, PA and later Middletown, OH. It was in the Middletown period that the famed racer Maldwyn Jones won a number of races on Flying Merkels. Around the beginning of WWI the brand was synonymous with high performance, but the shrinking market for motorcycles caused the company to close its doors in 1917.

Day 209:
Thor
In an early example of "outsourcing," Indian bought motors from Thor as early as 1903. The company later produced a fine V-twin of its own with inlet-over-exhaust cylinder heads. Thors produced from 6 to 9 horsepower, which was competitive at the time. Nonetheless, the company ceased production in 1916.

Day 210:

Holley

Beginning in 1902, George and Earl Holley began building motorcycles by mounting their interesting, rearward-facing engines in reinforced bicycle frames. The brothers were particularly skilled in the area of carburetor design and by 1908, Henry Ford had convinced them to supply carbs for his Model-T. Sometime in the 1910s, the Holleys gave up motorbikes to focus on supplying Ford with car parts.

Day 211:

Jefferson

Around 1910 Percy E. Mack started making PEM motorcycles. They were very good and were either copied or licensed by the Jefferson company, which improved the design still further. Beginning in 1911, Jeffersons were made with 499cc single-cylinder or 998cc V-twin motors. These were among the first motorcycles with both front and rear suspension. When Maldwyn Jones raced Flying Merkels, they were sometimes modified to run with Jefferson OHV cylinder heads. The company only lasted a few years, ceasing business in the same year the First World War began – 1914.

Day 212:

Morse-Beauregard

This company produced a 492cc vertical twin, with the cylinders in line with the frame and shaft drive. The firm began in Detroit in 1912 but moved to Buffalo. They produced under the name MB until 1920.

Gone and best forgotten – bikes we're better off without

Of course, many of bankrupt motorcycle companies failed for good reason – their bikes were dated, their quality was poor, their designs were ill-conceived, or they completely failed to understand their market. In fact, some of the companies on this list made all those mistakes at once. Here are ten bikes you might want in your collection, but you wouldn't want to ride!

Day 213:
Indian
Sacrilege! You say. It's true that between 1901 and 1955 Indian produced many of America's – maybe even the world's – best motorcycles. Fans of "the Wigwam" often bemoan the fact that Harley-Davidson was the company that survived as the lone American motorcycle maker.

But it's not great motorcycles like the Scout and Chief we're better off without, or even the Velocettes that Floyd Clymer imported as "Indians" in the early '60s. No, the nadir of the great Indian brand came after Clymer's death when his lawyer, Alan Newman, sold Taiwanese-made Indian *minibikes* in the back pages of 1970s pulp magazines. Hendee and Hedstrom must have turned over in their graves.

Day 214:

Cushman

The Cushman company of Lincoln, NE was in the lawnmower and utility engine business. In 1936, they decided to make scooters because they had more motors than they could sell.

During WWII, Cushman supplied U.S. paratroopers with a bizarre folding scooter that came in a crate intended to survive parachute drops. It was underpowered, had no suspension and very small wheels. In an airborne combat situation, it would be better if the parachute failed to open and it landed on the enemy. Paratroopers left them behind, and some were used for light courier duty on airbases.

Cushman made their last scooter in 1966, when it became apparent that they could not compete with the Honda step-through Cub for practicality or Vespa for style.

Day 215:

Lilac

In the 1950s and early '60s, American motorcycle enthusiasts criticized the Japanese motorcycle industry for shamelessly copying of European designs. In truth, some Japanese designs were pretty derivative. The Kawasaki K2 (later known as the W1) was a legal copy of the BSA A10, for example. But most BSAs leaked oil and were on balance no better than the Kawasaki.

Lilac was one of the first and best of the postwar Japanese motorcycle companies but it was also one of the first to fold, in 1961. It's mistake? Lilac chose to copy a great bike, the BMW.

Customers never really got over the fact that although it was good, it was nowhere near as well made as the real thing.

Day 216:
Bohmerland
These oddly advanced motorcycles were made in Czechoslovakia from 1927 until the start of WWII. Although most were powered by conventional 600cc single-cylinder motors, that was where convention ended as far as the designer, Albin Liebisch, was concerned.

With a wheelbase of around six feet, there was room for a very long saddle, intended for the rider and *two* passengers. Under Czech law, a motorcycle could carry no more than three people. However, a pair of fuel tanks were mounted above the rear wheel and those were often padded, providing room for two *additional* passengers – yes up to five people sitting one behind the other.

Day 217:
Megola
Like the Bohmerland, these are now highly sought after by collectors. But if the Czech bike is odd, this German machine is downright alien. It was powered by a 640cc five-cylinder radial motor *in the front wheel*. There was no clutch or gearbox, making it almost impossible to use in traffic – bringing the machine to a stop entailed stalling the motor. That niggling detail didn't prevent 2000 of the bikes being made and sold between 1921 and '25.

Day 218:
PER
Kurt Passow, a German, designed the Pawa in 1922. It was a very unique-looking motorcycle, with a bucket seat and fully enclosed bodywork – but it certainly wasn't fully thought out. After that commercial failure, Passow started a new company to make the PER, which also had elaborate bodywork made out of flat steel sheets. It looked rather like a two-wheeled armored personnel carrier, although it was in fact quite comfortable to ride.

Passow claimed that his 342cc two-stroke motor would run on anything from crude oil to turpentine but the problem was that it rarely ran at all. By 1926 he was out of the motorcycle business altogether.

Day 219:
Holden
Colonel H. Capel Holden, an Englishman, built the first four-cylinder motorcycle in 1897 or '98. His 3 horsepower creation was commendably compact but proportioned like a child's tricycle, with a big front wheel and a tiny rear one. The effect was remarkably ugly and Holden was out of the manufacturing business by 1903. He did do the sport of motorcycling a big favor, however: he built Brooklands, the world's first race-track.

Day 220:
Silk

Alfred Angus Scott made some very advanced
motorcycles powered by water-cooled two-stroke
motors. Although its heyday was in the 1920s, the
Scott motorcycle company continued to build bikes
into the '60s. When it finally closed, George Silk (a
motorcycle racer who had been a Scott apprentice)
picked up the torch.

Silk had an up to date frame made to his
specifications by Spondon, a highly respected maker
of racing frames, so the bike handled well. The
problem is, he persisted in using the Scott motor. It
might have been ahead of its time in 1920 but was
comically dated in the late '70s. He managed to sell
about 150 of them.

Day 221:
Militaire

This would have been a very innovative motorcycle
had it succeeded, as it is, it was simply weird. It was
long and low-slung. The driver sat in a chair and used
a steering wheel to turn it. It was fitted with
permanent "training wheels." Another car-like feature
was a reverse gear. Between 1911 and '17, no less
than eight companies in Cleveland, Buffalo,
Springfield and Bridgeport tried their hand at making
it. All failed, selling less than 100 Militaires in total.

Day 222:

Whizzer

These auxiliary motors were produced for bicycles beginning in 1939. Whizzer produced the Pacemaker in '48, which was the company's first bike-plus-motor combination. It even produced a few full-fledged motorcycles in the 1950s.

The motorcycles were flops, but Whizzer sold over 150,000 auxiliary motors. At first the company thought the bikes would be used by adult commuters but most of the buyers turned out to be kids. Soon enough, Whizzers were being advertised in comic books. The company lobbied state governments to ensure its products would be considered "bicycles."

Early models produced a modest 1.4 horsepower but by the late '50s, 3-horsepower Whizzer motors could propel a kid on a bike 40 miles an hour. That was much too fast for bicycle tires, coaster brakes, or children's judgment. A spate of serious accidents caused states to draft legislation setting minimum ages and/or requiring a motorcycle license to operate them. Seeing the writing on the wall (and on court dockets after a few lawsuits) the company stopped selling the motors in 1965 – though replicas are now on the market again.

"America's 'Must-Ride' Roads"

Considering the millions of miles of roads crisscrossing the U.S.A. and Canada, it's surprising that some motorcyclists guard their favorite roads as though they were military secrets.

Web sites like pashnit.com have helped to spread the word about obscure roads that offer great sport bike riding but there's more to life than canyon-carving. Check out roadtripamerica.com for everything from historic highways to scenic byways to knee-down twisties.

This selection of personal favorites ranges from roads just a few miles long to multi-day journeys. It includes roads suited to all types of bikes and riders, although one road is not even paved, so it's limited to adventurous riders on adventure bikes!

Please note: some of these roads are technically challenging. Know your limits, ride at your own pace and always, always stay in control. If you ever accidentally cross the centerline, call it a day before your riding buddies have to call you an ambulance.

Day 223:

Key Largo to Key West

This section of U.S. 1 is also called "Overseas Highway" – appropriate, as you'll literally ride over the sea for much of its 95-mile length, from the southern tip of the Florida mainland into the Caribbean. Depending on your mood, you can channel Ernest Hemingway or Jimmy Buffett.

Most Keys travelers start hitting the margaritas by noon but motorcyclists will be safer overdoing the other local vice: key lime pie. While there are few bends, the highway has one surprising elevation change as it soars over the shipping lane at Seven-Mile Bridge. When you reach the Lower Keys, stop for a final award-winning slice of pie at Pepe's Café and Steak House. They house motto, "…a fairly good place for quite a long while" perfectly captures the laid back (dare I say "low key"?) local vibe. Recommended bike: Cruiser.

Day 224:

The Tail of the Dragon

U.S. Highway 129 crosses the Tennessee-North Carolina border at Deal's Gap. This is the most famous riding road in the country. The 'Dragon packs 300+ bends, dozens of bikes and sports cars along with several cop cars, police motorcycles and highway patrol helicopters into just 11 miles of road. It's an entertaining scene on the weekend, though the serious riding is done weekdays – preferably in the shoulder seasons. The area even has a bikes-only campground-resort. Recommended bike: Sport bike. (www.tailofthedragon.com, www.dealsgap.com)

Day 225:
The Blue Ridge Parkway
You can thank the Great Depression for this fantastic road, which was built as part of the "New Deal" public works program. The Parkway stretches over 450 miles from Shenandoah National Park in Virginia south to Great Smoky Mountains N.P. in Tennessee. The road winds smoothly through incredible scenery. Even the ditches are nicely groomed, and it would make a perfect place to exercise a hardcore sport bike – if it wasn't so heavily policed. If you must ride aggressively, explore the roads that branch off the Parkway and head back down to the lowlands. Recommended bike: Touring.
(www.blueridgeparkway.org/)

Day 226:
The Cabot Trail
The Canadian province of Nova Scotia (on the Atlantic coast north of Maine) is a great motorcycle touring/sport-touring destination but the most rewarding riding is on Cape Breton Island, in the extreme north of the province. The Cabot Trail is the name of a 200-mile road that circumnavigates the North end of the island (that's right, north of north of north – so plan a midsummer or early-fall trip.) The road was hacked out of seaside cliffs. The scenery and local seafood are all spectacular and affordable. Recommended bike: Sport-touring or Adventure bike.
(www.tourcanada.com/cabottrl.htm)

Day 227:
Arkansas Highway 341

The tip-off that this is a great riding road is that if you do a Mapquest search for directions from Big Flat to Norfork, it suggests the much more traveled Highway 5. In fact, there's a shortcut up Highway 341. For about 20 winding miles, this road passes through Ozark National Forest – meaning there is little likelihood of coming upon cross traffic. Most of the other roads on this list are deservedly famous but the Ozarks are one of American motorcycling's best kept secrets. Ideal for: Sport bike, sport-tourer.

Day 228:
Route 66

Route 66, as the 1946 song tells us, "winds from Chicago to L.A.". Well, it did. The "Mother Road" was rendered obsolete by the development of the Interstate Highway system. It was broken up – at first administratively, into a dozens of state and interstate routes, then in many cases physically as abandoned stretches succumbed to Midwestern weather. But in recent years there's been an effort to re-designate the route. Several guidebooks are available that will help you find and ride the all the surviving pavement. Recommended bike: Touring. (www.national66.com)

Day 229:
Mount Palomar

Palomar is located about an hour NE of San Diego, off California state highway 76. There are two routes up the mountain; both date from the depression, when a large astronomical observatory was built on top of the mountain.

The two roads are the seven-mile county road S6 (known as the South Grade) and the 14-mile S7, or the East Grade. Both climb nearly 5,000 feet from highway 76.

The South Grade is covered by California's blanket 50 mph speed limit but it is so tight and twisting that you don't need to speed in order to drag your knees. The surface is good, traffic is light and the weather is almost always fantastic. There's even a great burger-and-shake place at the top. On weekends, the parking lot is crowded with sport bikes and a few thinly disguised track missiles but there are always a few cruisers, too. Everyone's welcome.

Day 230:
The Million-dollar Highway
This stretch of US550 connects the small towns of Ouray and Silverton, CO. It may only be 23 miles long but the roads to the Million-dollar Highway are all great riding roads in their own right, so in this case getting there is definitely half the fun. According to local legend, the highway got its name from the value of the silver ore used as fill during its construction. This road switchbacks up and down an 11,000 foot pass. Recommended bike: Sport-tourer.

Day 231:
Pacific Coast Highway
Highway 1 hugs the central California coast for several hundred miles, all of which offer great scenery and sinuous, gorgeous curves. Among

aficionados, the northernmost 40 or so miles from Fort Bragg up to Leggett are perhaps the most favored. This stretch is farther from the madding crowd. While Honda once named a touring bike after the PCH, it's popular with riders of everything from crotch rockets to choppers.

Day 232:
British Columbia's Stewart-Cassiar Highway
Touring up the Alaska Highway is an American rite of passage. But if you tire of passing hundreds of slow-moving motorhomes, there's an alternative road into the far north. Head west on Canada's Yellowhead Highway through the Rockies towards the British Columbia coastal town of Prince George. Then turn north on the legendary Highway 37 towards Watson Lake in the Yukon, where you'll rejoin the original Alaska Highway.

Highway 37 is a highway in name only. In reality, it is several hundred miles of very frost-heaved pavement with long gravel stretches. You'll take a pounding, but the reward is some of the most remote, rugged and beautiful scenery in the world. How remote is it, you ask? Put it this way, the highway occasionally doubles as a landing strip for bush planes. So look out for bears. And look up! Adventure bikes only, obviously.

Can't-miss events

There's more to motorcycles than racing. Here are ten annual events that every motorcyclist really must attend at least once in every lifetime – if not once a year!

Day 233:
Bike Week
This week-long blowout each March is the "official" start to the annual riding season in the U.S.A. While the claims of 350,000 bikers descending on Daytona FL are certainly exaggerated, there certainly are lots of bikes, loads of beer, and yes… babes. It used to be described as "Spring break at the penitentiary." It's a lot more controlled these days and if the number of gray beards is any indication, it will soon resemble Spring break at the old folks' home. (http://www.daytonachamber.com/)

Day 234:
Black Hills Motorcycle Classic
Better known simply as "Sturgis," this event's surpassed Bike Week as the largest gathering of motorcyclists in the U.S.A. (or for that matter, anywhere.) Whatever the case, enough bikers crowd this tiny town that the Midwestern press really don't need to exaggerate the attendance quite so wildly. Held in early August. It's not only for Harley riders. It's also for people who trailer their Harleys to the event. (www.sturgismotorcyclerally.com)

Day 235:
Laconia Motorcycle Week
This event is held each June in the New Hampshire lake country and is one of the oldest such "bike weeks" held in the U.S.A. The popular Weirs Beach camping area was the site of a full-fledged riot in 1965 but in recent years local officials have enforced a somewhat more family-friendly code of behavior. Now the event is supported with a substantial investment from the state government. (www.laconiamcweek.com)

Day 236:
Honda Hoot
What Sturgis is to the Harley cruiser set, the Hoot is to Gold Wing riders. As you might imagine, this event is much more laid-back and kid-friendly. Now well established in Knoxville TN. Held in late June. (www.hondahoot.com)

Day 237:
Femmoto
Only 53 people attended the first women-only track day in 2002. However it was an idea whose time had come and it has quickly blossomed. Now it's a multi-day "Lillith Fair" for women whose idea of music is revving engines. There are still track days, but there are also demo rides, gear displays and plenty of empowerment, both mechanical and metaphorical. So far, Femmoto events have been held in early October, in the Southwest. (www.femmoto.com)

Day 238:
Biketoberfest
If Bike Week (March) is too crazy for you, Daytona Beach's late-October event might be more your speed. Think of it as Bike Week Lite. The same (albeit often questionable) taste, with less alcohol. (www.biketoberfest.org)

Day 239:
AMA Vintage Motorcycle Days
Held every summer (usually in late July) at the Mid-Ohio Sports Car Course in Lexington OH. This three-day event includes a full slate of AHRMA racing, a massive swap meet, auction, and much more. (www.midohio.com)

Day 240:
Elephant Rally
OK, so this event is held in Germany and thus a little harder to get to. It's still crazy enough to be a "must" on this list. Every year in late January or early February, hundreds of motorcyclists ride to the famous Nurburgring race track and camp out over a weekend – usually in deep snow and subzero temperatures. Depending on which story you want to believe, the gathering gets its name from Hannibal's crossing of the Alps "mit elefanten," or from the green war-surplus Zunapp motorcycles (nicknamed elephants by German soldiers) that were used by many of the first campers when the event began in the '50s. (http://www.alteselefantentreffen.de/)

Day 245:
Vashon TT
Located in Puget Sound near Seattle, WA, the Isle of
Vashon hosts an annual poker run and gathering of
(mostly vintage) motorcycles in late summer. Since
the island can be reached only by ferry and capacity is
limited, the event's date is made known only to
members of the Vintage Motorcycle Enthusiasts. It's
well worth joining this great club, based in the Pacific
Northwest, just to find out when to head to Vashon.

Day 246:
Ralph Wayne's Vintage Backyard Nationals
This is literally a grassroots event – it is still held on
the organizer's back lawn – although it now attracts
over 5,000 motorcycles! Over the last 20 years, the
"Backyard Nationals" has become one of the premier
gatherings of old American and European
motorcycles, though all makes (and all riders) are
welcome. The event is held in early October in
Kansas City. One of the refreshing things about it is
that it's completely non-commercial: there are no
entry fees, no vendors, no sponsors and no hassles.
Oh, and every bike that enters wins a ribbon, so there
are no losers, either. (Info: Wayne's Motorcycle Sales
and Service 816-421 6950)

Museums and Collections

Next time you want to make points with your wife, offer to take the kids to a museum. Then head for any of these incredible motorcycle museums.

Day 247:
Barber Vintage Motorsports Museum
There may be debate about which one of these museums has the best collection, but there's no doubt which one is the best *museum*. Birmingham native George Barber set out to amass the world's most important collection of motorcycles in 1988. By 2005, he'd acquired 1,000-plus bikes.

Part of his collection was housed in a smaller museum in downtown Birmingham until 2003, by which time Barber had spent $60 million of his own money to erect a fabulous museum on the outskirts of the city. The Barber Vintage Motorsports Museum is set in a beautiful park that includes a world-class racetrack. All this is the property of a non-profit corporation – making it the largest philanthropic investment in the history of Alabama. Worth a trip all on its own, no matter how far away you might live. The museum also houses the largest private collection of Lotus cars in the world. (www.barbermuseum.org, 205-699 7275)

Day 248:
National Motorcycle Musuem
This great collection of bikes is also in Birmingham, though it's several thousand miles away in Birmingham, *England*. Motorcyclists around the world were horrified a few years ago when word spread that the museum had suffered a catastrophic fire. However, it's open for business again and better than ever. As one would expect, there's an emphasis on British machines – particularly those from the heyday of the British industry (1930-'60.) No motorcyclist should visit Britain without seeing this collection. (www.nationalmotorcyclemuseum.co.uk/)

Day 249:
Honda Collection Hall
Located in Suzuka, Japan. This used to be a semi-private collection open only to Honda employees and a privileged few outsiders by invitation only. Now it's open to the general public. The Hall exhibits some pretty prosaic stuff – power generators, for example – but there's an emphasis on Honda's mind-boggling engineering feats, such as their *five-cylinder* 125cc Grand Prix racers from the early '60s. Needless to say the display of Honda motorcycles and Formula 1 cars is comprehensive.

Suzuka is sort of a Disneyland for gearheads. It is a large amusement park that includes a race-track steeped in history. Most motorcycle racers agree that the Suzuka circuit (which was originally built by Honda as a test facility) is the most challenging of its kind. Seeing the collection and a race at Suzuka are definite "musts" for any motorcyclist visiting Japan. (http://world.honda.com/collection-hall/)

Day 250:
Motorcycle Hall of Fame and Museum
The American Motorcyclist Association's museum is located at the association's headquarters in Pickerington OH (a suburb of Columbus.) The museum has a permanent collection but the emphasis at the museum is on themed exhibits that change every few months. (www.motorcyclemuseum.org, 614-856 2222)

Day 251:
Harley-Davidson Company Museum
When it opened in 2008 the official Harley museum instantly became a major motorcycling destination. The Motor Company's collection of 400+ machines had long needed a home and a spectacular one has been designed by the renowned New York firm Pentagram.

The Museum development (on a 20-acre site near downtown Milwaukee) features exhibit space as well as a restaurant, café, retail shop, meeting space, special events facilities, and the company's archives. Elvis may have left the building, but his motorcycle will be on display in this one.

Day 252:
The Sammy Miller Musuem
This museum is located in New Milton, Hampshire, on the English south coast. It began as a few bikes on display in Sammy Miller's motorcycle dealership but has since swelled to hundreds of bikes in what he himself admits is "a hobby gone mad."

The rarity and provenance of these (mostly racing) models makes this one of the most prized collections in private hands. Interestingly, every motorcycle is in working order. Miller was a trials world champion in the '60s. Now, he is a white-haired older gentleman but he still regularly rides his most valuable bikes – and he's not afraid to *really* put them through their paces. Obviously, he too is still in perfect working order. (www.sammymiller.co.uk/)

Day 253:
Indian Motocycle Museum and Hall of Fame
Located in Springfield MA, in a building that was used by the Indian company until it ceased manufacturing in 1953. Note the idiosyncratic use of the term "motocycle" – that was the word Indian coined to describe their newfangled motorized bicycle in about 1901. They kept using it until they realized the rest of the world was determined to spell motorcycle with an "r." A great collection of old Indian motobikes and memorabilia. Other American makes are also represented. (413-737 2624)

Day 254:
Wheels Through Time
This very interesting private collection of American-made motorcycles and cars is on display in tiny Maggie Valley NC, near the town of Asheville. Dale Walksler is another museum owner who's not afraid to start 'em up and ride 'em, so you never know what you might hear roaring up and down the driveway. Visitors can also check in on several restorations in progress. (www.wheelsthroughtime.com)

Day 255:
Ducati Museum
If you promise your wife a romantic Tuscan vacation she won't begrudge you a day at the Ducati factory in Bologna. It might be a tenth the size of Harley's museum, but it is big enough to convey Ducati's oh-so-Italian passion. Other companies race so they can sell motorcycles, but at Ducati, they sell motorcycles so they can race. (www.ducati.com/heritage/)

Day 256:
Solvang Motorcycle Museum
This small, elegant museum (it's located in an old Brooks Brothers shop) displays an ever-changing selection of machines from the collection of Dr. Virgil Elings. The good doctor was a physicist with a head for business and a heart for motorcycles – particularly racers, as both he and his son are regular competitors on the AHRMA circuit.

Solvang is a quaint town in good riding country, on Highway 101 north of Los Angeles. Besides Dr. Elings' collection, Solvang is best known for Paula's, a really good pancake house on the main street. The collection is open weekends but weekday visitors are almost always accommodated by appointment. (www.motosolvang.com, 805-686 9522)

Amazing Comebacks

Mark Twain said "rumors of my death have been exaggerated." Motorcycling has seen some equally amazing comebacks... racers have returned from injury or obscurity and companies have come back from the brink.

Day 257:

Mike Hailwood's 1978 victory on the Isle of Man
"Mike the Bike" was widely recognized as the greatest motorcycle racer of all time, based on his Grand Prix racing exploits and many TT victories in the 1960s. With nothing left to prove on two wheels, he became a car racer. Although he won the world Formula 2 championship, his car career ended when he crashed a McLaren Formula One car at Nurburgring. That crash severely injured his legs.

Mike retired to New Zealand. Years later, he announced he would return to the Isle of Man. In the interim, motorcycles had changed a lot. There were many who feared the worst. In practice, Mike was not the youthful hero people remembered; he was bald, he limped, he looked older than his years. But come the TT Formula 1 race, he gave Ducati one of its most famous victories. He proved the adage, "old age and treachery will always defeat youthful enthusiasm" when he returned *again* in '79, winning a fourteenth TT before retiring once and for all.

Day 258:

Harley-Davidson nearly strikes out, then strikes it rich

In 1969, a controlling interest in Harley-Davidson was acquired by the American Machine and Foundry Company – previously known to most Americans only as a manufacturer of bowling equipment.

AMF's managers rolled a real gutter-ball. Harley-Davidson quality plummeted; dealers were forced to rebuild motors under warranty and magazines were brutally critical of test bikes. Used Harleys were described as "pre-AMF" in classified ads.

By 1980, sales were so bad that AMF planned to mothball the brand. A group of Harley executives led by Vaughn Beals bought the business. For the first time in years, they invested in R&D and quality control. The new "Evo" motor appeared in 1984, by which time H-D quality had hit levels not seen since the '40s.

If you were a baby boomer caught in a midlife crisis, you probably felt the urge to invest in a Harley. You'd've been better off buying company stock... $100 invested at the time of the 1986 IPO (with reinvestment of dividends) would have been worth $20,000 by 2003, when Harley celebrated its centenary!

Day 259:

Scott Russell's worst-to-first victory at Daytona

The 1995 Daytona 200 was set to be a battle between an American, Scott Russell, and an Englishman, Carl Fogarty. Pre-race trash talk reached levels more typical of playground basketball than motorcycle racing.

Russell crashed on the first lap, as Fogarty took off into the distance. Undaunted, Russell leapt over his crashed bike, picked it up and got restarted in dead last. Fogarty blamed a pace car incident for regrouping the field, but pace car or not, Russell passed over 60 bikes and won the race.

Day 260:

Barry Sheene

Sheene's near-mythical status was clinched when a BBC television crew happened to catch him in one of the scariest crashes of all time. He was testing a 3-cylinder Suzuki at Daytona when his rear tire failed at nearly 180 miles an hour. Sheene slid and tumbled for almost a mile while his machine disintegrated alongside him. He suffered a broken thigh, wrist and collarbone in the crash but amazingly was racing – and winning – again in six weeks.

In 1982 he smashed both legs (nearly severing one) in another horrific crash. Surgeons used 27 screws to repair that damage. Sheene again returned to Grand Prix racing although he never regained top form. He retired in 1985.

Day 261:
Doug Henry

After a stellar early career in AMA 125cc-class motocross, Henry – who was born in Milford, CT – moved up to the 250cc class in 1995. That year, at the Budd's Creek National event, Henry was locked in a battle with motocross legend Jeremy McGrath. Henry crashed hard and broke his spine. It was another crash that was captured by television cameras and it hurt just to watch it.

Henry was told he'd never race again but after an operation to fuse his shattered spine and a year in rehab, he was back on track. He won the 1998 AMA 250cc motocross championship and was later a stalwart competitor in the AMA Supermoto championship.

Day 262:
Triumph

This company would be better-named "Pheonix," considering the number of times it has risen from the ashes. After being merged with its old nemesis BSA in the early '50s, the BSA group was merged again to form Norton-Villiers-Triumph in 1973. By then, the British motorcycle industry was in a freefall. In the early '80s, a long and bitter labor dispute seemed to be the last straw as Triumph production ground to a few bikes a week.

In 1983, a real estate developer named Dennis Poore acquired Triumph's factory in Meriden (Leicestershire, England) and demolished it to build housing. Rather than let the Triumph name die, however, Poore built a new factory just a mile or two away in the town of Hinckley. After a shaky start, the company is again producing a full line of motorcycles marked by one of the most unique design philosophies in the industry.

Day 263:
MV Agusta
From the 1950s through the early '70s, MV Agusta dominated Grand Prix racing. Even mighty Honda never won the 500cc class championship while these fire-engine red Italian machines were racing. Sadly, the passion for winning died when the company founder Count Domenico Agusta died of a heart attack in 1971 and towards the end of that decade the company stopped making motorcycles altogether.

In 1995, an Italian industrialist named Claudio Castiglione bought the rights to the MV Agusta name. That could have been a cheap ploy to exploit a famous name, but Castiglione hired Massimo Tamburini – the designer of Ducati's esteemed 916 model – and gave him free rein. Tamburini's MV Agusta F4 first introduced in 1998 is thought by many to be the most beautiful motorcycle ever made.

Day 264:
Miguel Duhamel at Daytona, 1999
In 1998, Miguel Duhamel crashed in a rainy practice session for the AMA Superbike race in Loudon, NH. He slid across the wet track almost without slowing down at all and hit a concrete wall. He was left with a very severe compound fracture of the femur. Luckily for him, a famous orthopedic surgeon was at a nearby hospital giving a seminar to local doctors. Duhamel's

leg was repaired with a long metal rod and seven screws.

Duhamel is the son of Yvon Duhamel, a Canadian racing legend who was conspicuously fearless. It must run in the family. The following spring Miguel limped into Daytona on a cane. His crew had to lift him on and off his bikes. Nonetheless, he won both the 600cc Supersport race and the AMA 200 in 1999.

Day 265:
Four-stroke motors in Grand Prix racing
Until the 1960s, most high-performance motorcycles had four-stroke motors. Two-stroke motors were only used for cheap mopeds and scooters. Then Walter Kaaden, an East-German engineer, perfected the expansion chamber exhaust, instantly doubling the power of two-stroke motors. Within ten years, the four-stroke motor was obsolete in Grand Prix racing.

In 2003, the 500cc two-strokes that had been the premier class in the motorcycle World Championship were replaced by 990cc four-strokes. Traditionalists mourned the passing of the savage two-stroke 500s, which were replaced by the high-tech (and more rider-friendly) "MotoGP"-class.

Day 266:

Sam Wheeler

Sam built his first streamliner in 1958, with some friends from high school. In the mid-'60s he was drafted and sent to Viet Nam. "I'd given up land-speed racing because it was too dangerous," he once said "then I found myself *there*. I told myself, 'If I get out of here alive, I'm going to build another streamliner'."

Wheeler's first comeback was to return from Viet Nam in 1970 and build a Norton Commando-engined streamliner that went 207mph, a 750cc-class record. Then after more than a decade away from the Salt Flats, Wheeler came back *again* in '91 with a new machine. After *thirteen years* of coming back to the 'Flats every fall with that streamliner, Wheeler finally used it to set the outright land speed record for a two –wheeled vehicle when he was 64 years old. He went 332mph.

Best Motorcycle Movies

It's not surprising that the list of the best motorcycle movies of all time includes clusters of films made between the late '60s and early '70s, and again from 1995 to 2005. Those were the two periods in which postwar motorcycle sales – and interest in the sport of motorcycling – peaked.

Day 267:
On Any Sunday (1971)
Documentary filmmaker Bruce Brown was a surfer who made the classic '60s surf-doc "Endless Summer". Commercial success is rare in documentary films, but revenues from that one hit allowed Brown to retire young. He spent much of his time riding dirt bikes in California. Eventually he realized that bike racing was a perfect subject for another film. With investment from Steve McQueen, Brown's camera crews followed AMA Grand National contender Mert Lawill and versatile off-road racer Malcolm Smith, with cameos from McQueen himself. Flat out the best documentary film ever on the subject of motorcycle racing. The on-board camerawork at flat track races is superb – all the more impressive considering the size and weight of the cameras that were used!

Day 268:
Easy Rider (1969)

This film was written and produced by Dennis Hopper and Peter Fonda, who also starred in it. They play a pair of hippies who ride their choppers from L.A. to New Orleans. Along the way, they meet a cast of characters that includes an ACLU lawyer played by an unheralded Jack Nicholson.

The film was a true road movie, as the crew followed Fonda and Hopper (both avid riders in real life) as they crossed the American west picking film locations on the spur of the moment. The narrative brilliantly captured the country's Vietnam-era malaise, and Hopper was acclaimed as the best new director at the Cannes Film Festival. Fonda's "Captain America" chopper became an American icon. Interestingly, the bike disappeared after the film was completed.

Day 269:
Electra Glide in Blue (1973)

Half road film, half film noir, this cult classic tells the story of a vertically-challenged motorcycle cop (played by Robert Blake, whose real life was also plenty 'noir'). Blake's character, "Big John", wants to get off his bike and become a detective so he can work with his brain and not "sit on my ass getting calluses." This was the only film James Guercio ever directed; he's better known as a Grammy Award-winning producer, composer, and performer who worked with the jazz-fusion bands Blood, Sweat and Tears, and Chicago.

Day 270:

Dust to Glory (2005)

If the name Dana Brown rings a bell, it's because he's Bruce "On Any Sunday" Brown's son. Following in his dad's footsteps, Dana made this documentary about the Baja 1000 desert race in Mexico. The race is for cars and trucks as well as motorcycles but in the best family tradition, the emphasis is on motorcycle racer "Mouse" McCoy. Unlike his dad, Dana had access to 55(!) cameras and four helicopters, allowing him to capture the best footage ever of this epic race. Warning: Don't watch this film unless you have been inoculated against the racing bug. The Baja 1000 is one of the last races that's open to anyone and has classes allowing almost any vehicle to compete, so you won't have the "I don't have a racing license," or the "My bike's not legal for the event" excuses!

Day 271:

Continental Circus (1969)

Continental Circus documents a season in Grand Prix racing. This classic bit of cinema-verite is hard to find but well worth looking for. It was originally made in French by producer-director Jerome Laperrousaz, but it can also be found with English voice-over narration.

Laperrousaz follows a charismatic Australian privateer named Jack Findlay. The film brilliantly captures the end of an era – the last time when an independent racer with a couple of bikes slung in the back of his van could mix it up with world champions like Giacomo Agostini. Jack travels from country to country, sleeping in a tent at the track, and living from prize check to prize check. A trippy rock score reinforces the oh-so-'60s vibe. This is Woodstock, with gasoline instead of acid and plaster casts instead of long hair.

Day 272:
World's Fastest Indian (2005)
This film was written and directed by Roger Donaldson. It is based on a true story about Bert Munro, an eccentric New Zealander who traveled to the Bonneville Salt Flats in order to prove that he had the world's fastest Indian motorcycle. Along the way Munro meets a cast of characters nearly as charming and offbeat as he is. The film stars Anthony Hopkins.

Day 273:
Crusty Demons of Dirt (1995)
In the early '90s the aptly named Fleshwound Films company – which had already made a couple of successful extreme snowboarding videos – turned its cameras on motorcyclists in the deserts of SoCal and Nevada. Fleshwound spent two years filming established Supercross stars like Jeremy McGrath and Jeff Emig, as well as then-unknown freeriders like Brian Deegan, Mike Metzger and long-jump lunatic Seth Enslow. They set their footage to an indie-thrashmetal soundtrack and created a video that launched the whole "freeride" FMX phenomenon.

Day 274:
The Motorcycle Diaries (2004)
Based on Che Guevara's own account of his journey
through Latin America on an old Norton. If you're
watching it as a motorcyclist and not a budding
communist, you'll probably find the second half of
the film, after Che abandons his bike, to be less
entertaining than the first half. However, intelligent
direction by Brazilian director Walter Salles and a
typically fine performance by Mexican actor Gael
Garcia Bernal made this film a darling of awards
juries everywhere. It even won an Oscar for Best
Original Song, "Al Otro Lado Del Rio" by composer
Jorge Drexler.

Day 275:
One Man's Island (2003)
If documentaries like On Any Sunday or Dust to
Glory are sweeping, One Man's Island is intimate and
intensely personal. Canadian independent director
Peter Riddihough spent the better part of a year
following an ordinary rider who quit his job and sold
all his possessions in order to move to the Isle of Man
and race in the famous TT. It's a film about
motorcycle racing that non-racers can also appreciate
since, at its heart, it's a story about the pursuit of
dreams.

Worst motorcycle movies of all time

On one hand it's easy to compile a list of terrible bike flicks – after all, the list of *bad* motorcycle movies is almost identical to the list of *all* motorcycle movies. The good ones are the exceptions.

On the other hand, with so many real stinkers to choose from, narrowing the field to the ten worst is tricky. Some of them are so bad they're almost amusing. (Note that I said "almost"– watching them is still painful.) The following ten is a strictly personal list including films that are about motorcycling, as well as a few films in which bikes play notably lame supporting roles.

Day 276:
The Wild One (1953)
This film was almost certainly the most influential motorcycle movie of all time – unfortunately it influenced America to hate and fear motorcyclists! Laszlo Benedek directed a star-studded cast including Lee Marvin and, of course, Marlon Brando.

Thanks to Brando, this movie's still in every Blockbuster store but don't kid yourself – it's as dated as stale cheese. The outlaw bikers come across more like disaffected artists from the Left Bank in Paris and as for Brando's performance… let's just say that it's no "On the Waterfront." Benedek made the film shortly after emigrating from Europe. Once he was more settled in California, he was a solid Emmy contender as a TV director, but this movie stinks!

Day 277:
No Limit (1936)
This movie was a huge hit in prewar Britain and definitely consolidated the TT's status as the world's most important motorcycle race. It starred George Formby, who was a ukelele-playing vaudeville star and enormously popular as a live performer. He plays a speed demon determined to win the TT on a motorcycle of his own design. How this movie managed to become a box office success and survive to this day on video is a complete mystery. The race action is almost comically bloodthirsty, Formby's off-key singing grates on your ears, and as an actor he made Stan Laurel look like Sir Laurence Olivier.

Day 278:
The Wild Angels (1966)
Saying that this film is about a couple of Hells Angels facing off against the cops is misleading, as there's practically no plot. That was one of its many flaws, which prompted film critic Christopher Null to call it "truly one of the most awful films ever made."

It's perhaps even more tragic in that many of the people involved had real talent and/or Hollywood Boulevard street cred. The movie was directed by B-movie "auteur" Roger Corman. His (massive) oeuvre is now being reappraised by serious film critics. Peter Bogdanovich worked on the screenplay. Peter Fonda, Bruce Dern, and Nancy Sinatra starred in it. The film opened at the prestigious Venice Film Festival. Don't kid yourself: none of that comes close to saving it.

Day 279:
The Hellcats (1967)
"Motorcycle mamas on a highway to Hell!" "Leather on the outside... All woman on the inside!" This movie was luridly promoted as the story of a bike gang run by women. It's notable mainly for its comically bad post-production; in some shots motorcycles approach in utter silence, while other scenes with no bikes have loud motor sound effects. Director Robert Slatzer had a thankfully brief career as a cheap, exploitive sensationalist. Sadly it didn't end soon enough to protect the world from "Hellcats."

Day 280:
Biker BoyZ (2003)
For the last twenty years at least, the whole urban/African-American/outlaw street-racing scene has been rich fodder for a great action film... too bad no one has made it. Real street racers will marvel at the scene in which a couple of turbo- and nitrous-modified Hayabusas stage a drag race on a gravel road.

Day 281:
Torque (2004)
Another take on the street-racing scene, this time complicated by the tired old framed-for-murder plot device. Curiously, director Joseph Kahn came to this project having done almost nothing but Britney Spears videos.

Day 282:
Supercross (2005)
The colorful world of professional Supercross racing forms the backdrop for this limping story in which two brothers have a falling out. They become bitter rivals before hardship brings them back together. Cue: audience rolls eyes.

This movie is the only directorial effort by Steve Boyum, an established Hollywood stunt coordinator. It has quite possibly the least-talented cast and crew in the history of cinema, but it's Boyum himself who's most to blame for its box office failure. Real supercross is so spectacular that it doesn't need stunts at all – let alone a stunt coordinator as director. Someone capable of telling a compelling story could probably make a great movie about this sport but, the way Hollywood works, *Supercross's* flop will make it impossible to pitch another SX script for at least a few more years.

Day 283:
I Bought a Vampire Motorcycle (1990)
By day it's a Norton sitting quietly in a garage. But by night it is possessed by a demon and emerges to drink the blood of anyone foolish enough to act in this film, er, wait a minute, I meant to write "walk around Birmingham after dark". Plenty of splattered gore and – I'm not making this up – a talking turd. Even stranger than that last tidbit is the fact that director Dirk Campbell was previously known as the writer-director of *Country Diary of an Edwardian Lady*. Surely those are the two most divergent films ever made by a single person.

Day 284:
Special industry award: American Chopper (c. 2005)
No one was more surprised than the Discovery Channel when the Teutels' dysfunctional family schtick became the network's most-watched show. In short order it spawned a host of imitators. The real problem is that millions of Americans watch them and actually think, "This is real." In fact, Hollywood screenwriters are up in arms because the writers who work on such "reality" shows are paid far less than those who write for shows like "Lost" or even "Joey".

Why, you might wonder, would reality TV even *need* writers? That's a good question. In 2005, at least 1,200 members of the Writer's Guild of America worked in the reality genre. Clearly they weren't all writing hosts' introductions and voice-over narration. You don't suppose the Teutels' tantrums are *scripted?*

Day 285:
Dopey-stunt award (tie) Matrix Reloaded (2003)
Mission: Impossible 2 (2000)
The breathless advance promotion of both of these films emphasized the ludicrous claim that Carrie-Ann Moss and Tom Cruise both did their own stunts. If only that were true! Both would've been killed early in production and we would have been spared these tiresome sequels.

In fact, the Wachowski brothers'* signature "stunting" is mostly done in computerized post-production. That explains why real motorcyclists find Trinity's Ducati ride through oncoming traffic to be visually spectacular but fundamentally unconvincing. At least Mission: Impossible's old-school action film director John Woo still arranges for most of his stunts to be done in front of the camera. Real riders will note that Ethan's tires change from knobbies (when he's riding on dirt or gravel) to slicks (when he's riding on pavement) in the same chase sequence. If the villain could simply patent those tires, he wouldn't have to threaten the release of a deadly virus in order to hold the world for ransom.

(*They're not brothers any more: Larry Wachowski became 'Lana' after a sex-change.)

The best – and best-selling – books on bikes

Thousands of books have been published on motorcycle subjects, but most of them are technical manuals or uncritical photo histories of specific brands. If you only want to devote a foot or two of shelf space to motorcycle titles, here's my personal selection. Some of these titles were critically acclaimed best sellers, some are niche titles known only to devoted motorcyclists. All are insightful and authoritative.

Day 286:
The Art of the Motorcycle
This exhibit was the biggest hit ever for the Guggenheim Museum in New York. Later, it toured and set records at Chicago's Field Museum and the Guggenheim in Bilbao, Portugal. For many people, "The Art of the Motorcycle" signified the coming of age of motorcycling. The exhibit was accompanied by this massive, hardbound catalog lavishly illustrated with color photos. Coffee table book nothing; you could attach legs to this tome and *use it* as a coffee table.

Day 287:
Zen and the Art of Motorcycle Maintenance
Robert Pirsig submitted this epic tale to 121 publishers who all rejected it. The 122nd, William

Morrow, accepted it and offered their minimum advance: $3000. It went on to sell millions of copies in dozens of languages – making it by far the most successful book ever about motorcycles.

Day 288:
Hells Angels
This was the book that launched Hunter S. Thompson's career as a gonzo journalist. Any suggestion of cool detachment was destroyed right on the front cover, which trumpeted it as "A strange and terrible saga." Thompson spent a lot more time hunched over a bar with a stiff drink in front of him than over the handlebars of a motorcycle in the company of Hells Angels but this book still includes really vivid descriptions of motorcycle riding. Few books have done that as well before or since.

Day 289:
Illustrated Encyclopedia of Motorcycles
Czech motorcycle historian Erwin Tragatsch compiled an amazing database on hundreds of motorcycle brands – many of which were produced for only a few years. His encyclopedia is no longer in print but can still be found in bargain bins and used bookstores. If you see it, grab it. It's the definitive guide to virtually every motorcycle made before 1980. An updated edition was released in 2000, with additional content compiled by Kevin Ash. That book is still in print.

Day 290:
The Art of Motorcycle Racing

Mike Hailwood was the greatest motorcycle rider of his generation – many would say of all time. In 1963, he published this book, co-written by Murray Walker, the almost equally famous BBC broadcaster.

Like many naturally gifted athletes, Mike found his skills difficult to describe. However, his book provides advice on riding and racecraft that is still useful, as well as insight into his personality and life as the biggest star during the golden age of Grands Prix. Out of print and highly collectible; if you find a copy for less than $100, buy it on the spot.

Day 291:
A Twist of the Wrist

As founder of the California Superbike School, Keith Code can probably claim to be the dean of riding coaches. This book outlines the CSS program and although the emphasis is on sport bikes, it has much to offer riders of all motorcycles. If you're going to buy one book on riding technique, this would be a good choice.

Day 292:
The Perfect Vehicle

This memoir by Melissa Holbrook Pierson was published by the tony W.W. Norton company in 1998 and got rave reviews in all the best newspaper book sections – probably the first time in 25 years (since "Zen and the Art…") that any motorcycle title had received such widespread acceptance. Pierson mixes a motorcycle narrative with a vaguely creepy love story. The book is written from a decidedly feminine perspective but it can be enjoyed by men, too. (Especially members of the Moto Guzzi cult.) Disappointingly, Pierson didn't prove to be a lifelong motorcyclist... she abandoned two wheels and took up horseback riding for her next book and never looked back.

Day 293:
The Motorcycle Diaries: Notes on a Latin American Journey

Ernesto "Che" Guevara became a socialist hero and a counter-culture icon, despite his early bourgeois upbringing in Argentina. As a young man, he took a months-long trip on an aging Norton motorcycle. Along the way, Che learned something every motorcyclist learns – travel on two wheels puts you in much closer contact with the people and places you travel through. Thus the motorcycle introduces Che to poverty and injustice in Latin America, and setting him on the road to becoming a Communist revolutionary.

Day 294:
Riding Man

This book sets out to answer the question "why on earth would anyone race motorcycles". Seeking the answer, the author moves to the Isle of Man to experience the only place in the world where motorcycles are central to local culture, and not a subculture. Ultimately, the real question becomes "why pursue your dreams, whatever they are?"

Day 295:
Daytona 200: The history of America's premier motorcycle race
Don Emde is a former winner of the 200 and an experienced historian of motorcycle racing as well. As the subtitle implies, the study of this race opens a window on the history of American motorcycling as a whole.

Feats of endurance

Until you've tried riding a thousand or more miles a day for days or weeks at a stretch, it's hard to see why anyone would bother ranking or rating feats of simple endurance. Still, for a lot of riders, it's not about getting your knee down in the corners or doing a perfect nac-nac off a big jump, it's about grinding out the miles. And miles. And miles.

In the U.S., there's an "official" governing body for endurance attempts – the aptly named Iron Butt Association (www.ironbutt.com). The 24,000-member IBA has held its 11-day, 11,000-mile Iron Butt Rally every couple of years since 1984. In recent years there have typically been about 100 entries and a surprising 90% of riders have finished. Here are some highlights from the IBA record books and if reading them isn't enough to give you saddle sores, another handful of amazingly arduous adventures.

Day 296:
Highest mileage in an Iron Butt Rally
Each rider chooses his own route between checkpoints, so mileages vary. George Barnes, a BMW rider from Colorado has twice put in over 13,000 miles over the 11 days.

Day 297:
Most Iron Butt Finishes
Harold Brooks, a Gold Wing rider from Virginia has finished five times. BMW motorcycles have been used to score more IBR finishes than any other brand.

Day 298:
Oldest rider with an Iron Butt
The oldest rider ever to finish was Garve Nelson, a Californian who rode a Honda Pacific Coast. He was 69 when he finished the 1993 Iron Butt. He would have finished again at the age of 71 in '95 but he was disqualified for providing illegal assistance to another competitor.

Day 299:
Best female with an Iron Butt
Only about a dozen female riders have finished the rally. Fran Crane, a Californian riding a BMW K100 was the best of them, coming second in 1987.

Day 300:
Oddest and oldest bikes to finish an IBR
In 2001, Keith Keating (Florida) rode a twelve-horsepower Suzuki GN125 commuter bike over 8,000 miles to score his finish. The bike was completely

stock and needed no repairs of any kind. That same year, Leonard Aron (California) finished on his 1946 Indian Chief.

Day 301:
Simon says, ride
Between 1973 and '77, Ted Simon (England) rode his 500cc Triumph Tiger 100 twin nearly 80,000 miles on a 'round-the-world trip. He nicknamed the bike Jupiter, and wrote an account of his journey titled "Jupiter's Travels." It's good reading and one could easily argue that it deserves a place on the list of the 10 best motorcycle books. Jupiter (the motorcycle, not the planet) is on permanent display in the National Motorcycle Museum in Birmingham, England – a museum that *is* on my 'best museums' list.

Day 302:
That's not an iron butt. *This* is an iron butt
In 1983, Keith Kimber and Tania Brown (England) bought a Honda CX500. The couple planned a four year world tour. They were gone for 17 years, wandering across six continents and through 98 countries.

Keith and Tania used 13 front and 18 rear tires. The resourceful Kimber built his own luggage rack and used Zarges Hobby Boxes for luggage. He cut down ammunition boxes to hold his tools and built strong crash bars to protect the CX500's engine. (As a transverse V-twin, the cylinders stick out at the sides and are vulnerable.) He typically carried four two-and-a-half gallon jerry cans, two filled with fuel and two with fresh water. He made wire mesh screens to protect the radiator and headlight. Tania used the headlight screen to grill burgers over many campfires.

Day 303:
Cape-to-Cape by Cub
Adam Paul of Chester, England rode a Honda Super Cub (C90) step-through scooter from Cape Horn (Argentina) to the Cape of Good Hope (South Africa) via Alaska and Siberia. The 36,640-mile trip took two years, from 1996-'98.

Day 304:
And the McGyver Award goes too...
Klaus Schubert and Claudia Metz, who planned a "short" ride from their home in Germany to Japan on their Yamaha XT500 trail bikes. They didn't come back for 16 years. The pair covered about a quarter of a million kilometers, showing conspicuous ingenuity. Once when they ran out of gas in the desert, they lashed the bikes together and rigged them with a sail. Incredibly, they used their motorcycles for most of the water crossings, too – they built rafts from found materials and scrap, then rigged up paddle wheels powered by the bikes! One such raft is now on permanent display in a German museum.

Day 305:
If their butts are iron, this guy's is stainless steel
In 1985, Emilio Scotto of Argentina set out from Buenos Aires on his trusty Honda Gold Wing and circumnavigated the globe. When he got back, he turned around and did it *again* in the opposite

direction. In ten years on the road he covered nearly half a million miles, filled 11 passports with visas and entry stamps, and used about 90 tires. His girlfriend traveled to India, where they were married in a Hindu ceremony. She then joined him on his journey as a passenger. For her sake, I hope she met up with him on his *second* lap.

Hell, hell, the gang's all here – Outlaw myth and reality

There will always be non-motorcyclists, your in-laws for example, who think anyone who rides – even a Vespa scooter or a Honda Gold Wing – is bent on rape and pillage. If you're to convince them otherwise, you'll need a few facts on your side.

So what do you need to know about the Hells Angels? Well for starters, they do exist, and if you back over one of their choppers, you should immediately leave the scene. And the country.

Seriously, the odds of that happening are small because there are a fewer Hells Angels than you think. Here's a factoid on their estimated worldwide membership and nine other things you'd rather learn from this book than from personal experience.

Day 306:
A Hells Angels census
Police intelligence reports suggest that there are about 230 Hells Angels chapters in pretty much every state and dozens of countries around the world. Despite this global presence, the club has only about 3,000 full members. Part of their outsized reputation stems from the fact that most of their dirty work is done by a far larger number of bikers trying to curry favor and earn their "colors."

Day 307:
Hells Angels, Inc.
The Hells Angels Motorcycle Corporation Inc. was incorporated in the state of California in 1970. The company's head office is in Oakland. The even have a web site, www.hells-angels.com.

Day 308:
About the name
The original Hells Angels club was founded in San Bernardino, CA in 1948. It took its name from a WWII B-17 bomber squadron. In the early years, it really was just a motorcycle club – it was even sanctioned by the American Motorcycle Association.

Day 309:
A subsidiary of Hells Angels, Inc.
Like other global companies, the Angels have subsidiaries. The largest of these is a club called the Nomads, which itself has chapters scattered around the world. Over the years there have been a few legitimate motorcycle clubs with this name, so to avoid confusion the Angels' subsidiaries have taken to calling themselves "Hells Angels Nomads" or "HAMC Nomads." The other major Angels subsidiary is group called the Red Demons.

Day 310:
Hells Angels™
The club sued the Walt Disney Corporation over misuse of its name and winged death's head logo. The alleged trademark infringement concerned the Disney film "Wild Hogs," the story of a group of middle-

aged suburban Harley riders (including Tim Allen) that runs afoul of a biker gang. The Hells Angels fighting with *lawyers*? What's this world coming to?

Day 311:
Hells Angels(sic)
Yes, there seems to be a missing apostrophe. Hey, they're outlaw bikers, not grammarians. A Hells Angel once hilariously "explained" the error by saying, "There's more than one Hell."

Day 312:
They're just a club. In the same way the mob exists mainly to play *bocce*
The Hells Angels and other motorcycle gangs are involved in the manufacture and distribution of drugs (notably methamphetamines,) illegal weapons sales, prostitution, protection rackets, vehicle theft (especially motorcycles,) etcetera.

One reason few full members of the Angels are convicted of such crimes is that, as with the Mafia, the dirty work is done by underlings with few direct connections to the gang.

Day 313:
The Laughlin River Run melee
The River Run, which is held every spring in Laughlin, Nevada, is one of the largest motorcycle rallies in the U.S.. Most participants are registered Republicans who only strive to *look* like outlaws without actually being outlaws. But in 2002 a gun and knife fight broke out between the Hells Angels and a gang called the Mongols in the Harrah's casino.

Presumably a Mongol was at some Angels' favorite slot machine.

Three people were killed and dozens were injured. In a related incident, a Hells Angel was shot a few hours later in San Bernardino county. Incredibly, considering the extensive video surveillance in the casino, only one person, a Hells Angel from Arizona, was charged. Those charges were eventually dropped.

Day 314:
They're #2, they try harder
The fastest growing bike gang in the U.S. may well be the Bandidos (aka Bandido Nation.) They were formed in 1966 in Texas and now have over 30 chapters and 500 members in the U.S. and Canada.

The Bandidos logo is a parody of the "Frito Bandito" advertising character. One presumes that Frito-Lay was too preoccupied with its 1965 merger to Pepsico to remember to file a lawsuit. The little bandit with the big sombrero and yard-long machete may be laughable, but the Bandidos are not funny – they're conspicuously violent, even by the standards of outlaw bikers.

Day 315:
To learn more, read...
Under and Alone, by William Queen. The author was an ATF agent who spent over two years undercover as a member of the Mongols (the same California outlaw gang that fought the Hells Angels in Laughlin.)

Warner Bros. had a film of this story in development, with Mel Gibson tipped to play the undercover agent, but I never hear that it came out.

Maybe that was because studio executives realized that after stories of Gibson's holocaust denial went public, along with threatening phone messages to his former girlfriend, audiences would never believe he was any better than the bikers he was supposed to be busting. The question for Warner Bros.' lawyers is, has the company acquired the rights to the Mongols' trademark?

Clubs and Organizations

For a bunch of rugged individualists, motorcyclists certainly seem to join a lot of clubs! By joining one or more of the clubs below, you can increase motorcycling's political clout, find riders who share your interests, and maybe even find that last part you need to restore your '64 Yakazuki trailbike.

Day 316:
American Motorcyclist Association
The AMA is the most important club for American riders. AMA membership is required for many types of competition, but the AMA is not all about – or even mostly about – racing. It's also the most important lobbying organization on behalf of motorcyclists, at all levels of government. AMA clubs organize hundreds of non-competitive events all over the country. Every American motorcyclist should visit the AMA headquarters in Pickerington, Ohio at least once; it's the site of a great museum and the national motorcycle Hall of Fame. Members receive a monthly magazine to keep track of it all. If you join one organization, this should be it. (www.ama-cycle.org, 1-800 AMA JOIN)

Day 317:
Motorcycle Safety Foundation
The MSF is by far the most important source of basic
motorcycle street riding instruction in the U.S.A. The
organization's RiderCourse training certificate is
accepted in place of the motorcycle road skills test by
most states. If you or someone you know is just
getting started, taking an MSF course is the first step
towards a lifetime of safe riding. Joining the MSF and
becoming an instructor or rider-coach is also a great
way for experienced riders to give back to their
community. (www.msf-usa.org, 1-800 446 9227)

Day 318:
Women's International Motorcycle Association
WIMA may not be the oldest women's riding
organization (that honor probably goes to the Motor
Maids) but it's definitely where the cool chicks hang
out. Women who join WIMA get to take advantage of
a worldwide network of female riders, which is
especially useful if you plan to ride in foreign
countries. (www.wimausa.org)

Day 319:
ABATE
Depending on which state you live in, ABATE could
stand for anything from "American Bikers Aimed
Towards Education," to "A Brotherhood Against
Totalitarian Enactments." Much of ABATE's energy
seems to be devoted to lobbying for the rights of
motorcyclists to ride without helmets; it's as if the
National Rifle Association lobbied primarily to allow
gun owners to play Russian roulette.

Day 320:
Championship Cup Series
CCS unites grassroots racing clubs at tracks across the country. If you've got an itch to learn just how fast your bike is, the street is no place to scratch it. Getting an amateur race license is easy, far safer, and – in the long run – much cheaper. The first step is contacting CCS. (www.ccsracing.com, 817-246 1127)

Day 321:
American Historic Racing Motorcycle Association
AHRMA organizes races of all types for vintage motorcycles. Racing old bikes is as fun as racing contemporary bikes but often cheaper and less intimidating than sharing practice sessions with fearless 20 year-olds on 180-hp ZX-10s! Even if you don't plan on racing, AHRMA members are a great resource if you're restoring an old bike. (www.ahrma.org, 810-225 085)

Day 322:
Antique Motorcycle Club of America
With chapters across the U.S.A., this club brings together anyone interested in restoring or riding bikes over 35 years of age. (www.antiquemotorcycle.org)

Day 323:
H.O.G. – The Harley Owner's Group
With nearly a million members around the world, this may well be the biggest motorcycle club of all. Almost every Harley-Davidson dealership is home to a chapter and almost every chapter organizes all kinds

of events ranging from parking lot weenie roasts to charity rides to transcontinental treks. H.O.G. members also get preferential treatment when it comes to the rental of Harley motorcycles, too. (www.hog.com)

Day 324:
Honda Riders Club of America
If you've recently purchased a Honda motorcycle, you probably already are a member of the HRCA. Members receive Red Rider magazine, discounts at a number of riding schools, access to special parking at motorcycle races and invitations to all sorts of events and group rides. (www.hrca.honda.com, 800-847 HRCA)

Day 325:
Other owner's clubs
Although H.O.G. and HRCA are the two most-active owner's clubs, several other manufacturers sponsor similar groups. While most of these clubs are less event-driven than the two mentioned above, there are benefits to joining – often including roadside assistance.
ROK – Riders of Kawasaki (www.kawasaki.com/gtoc/, 877-ROK CLUB)
DOC – (Ducati) Desmo Owners Club (www.ducati.com/ducatiworld/clubs/home.jsp)
BMW Motorcycle Owners of America (www.bmwmoa.org, 636-394 7277)

Best places for motorcyclists to live

These cities all have vibrant bike scenes. They offer great bike shops, and bike-friendly bars and cafes. They're near good riding roads and have great local tracks. And although it's hard to quantify, they have a positive attitude about motorcycles as evidenced by things like motorcycle-only parking. Some of these cities also boast a number of motorcycle-related businesses, so if you do move to one of them you might even get a job in the motorcycle industry.

Day 326:

San Francisco, CA

It's no accident 'Frisco is America's best city for motorcycles – the traffic is so bad only motorcycles can move through it and the parking is worse! Maybe that's why there are twice as many bikes registered there, per capita, as in Los Angeles. People ride every kind of bike in the Bay Area; downtown it's a hotbed of vintage Vespas and mopeds, but across the bay in Oakland you're in chopper country.

Mainly though, San Franciscans favor sport bikes. The more exotic – or the rattier – the better. Munroe Motors is one of the country's biggest MV Agusta dealers. At the other end of the spectrum but in the same south-of-Market area, you'll find Moto Java, a funky café/accessory/used bike shop.

The coastal mountains and Napa wine country have great roads. The local racing club, the American Federation of Motorcyclists, has been around longer than the AMA. Its home track, Infineon Raceway, is just north of the Golden Gate Bridge. Race fans that live in the Bay Area can watch the USGP at nearby Laguna Seca without paying outrageous Monterey hotel bills, too.

In spite of wet winters and foggy summers, a lot of Bay Area riders rely on their bikes for day-to-day transportation, year 'round. As a result, local car drivers watch out for motorcyclists and the city takes a live-and-let-live approach to motorcycle parking.

Day 327:
Atlanta, GA
This city is home to the U.S. importers of Triumph motorcycles and Maxxis Tires. The almost unbearably hip Vortex café in the Little Five Points neighborhood has one of the country's most diverse and well attended weekly bike nights. Road Atlanta, home of Kevin Schwantz' racing school and an AMA Superbike doubleheader weekend is an hour north. Talladega is an hour to the East and if Atlantans want to ride two hours, they can also catch AMA Superbike action at Barber Motorsports Park and visit the world's best motorcycle museum.

Day 328:
San Diego, CA
It might be a coincidence that San Diego has produced more Daytona 200 winners than any other city, but it certainly has the best riding weather in the

country. The area is home to a host of motorcycle businesses including the two best suppliers of race bodywork, Catalyst Racing Composites and Air-Tech, as well as the cool clothing company Icon.

Café Calabria in North Park, imports and roasts its own coffee, serving the best brew south of Seattle. It always has a few cool bikes parked in front of it – or even inside it! On any Sunday, the streets of Julian, a quaint town an hour's ride away, are lined with cruisers. Hundreds of motorcyclists socialize as they walk off a slice of famous Julian apple pie.

Day 329:
Milwaukee, WI
As the home of Harley Davidson, Milwaukee has more citizens employed in the motorcycle industry than any other American city. While it's true that Wisconsin has a long "off season," local bikers can pass some of those cold winter weekends in the Harley-Davidson museum.

Surprisingly though, Milwaukee's not all Harleys, all the time. Road America, one of the country's top tracks, is an hour away. The outlying town of Saukville definitely doesn't suck for sport bike riders – it's home to Corse Superbikes, which is one of the best dealers anywhere for those *other* famous V-twins… Ducatis.

Day 330:
Columbus, OH
The AMA heaquarters are located in the Columbus suburbs. That makes it the home of the Motorcycle Heritage Museum and Hall of Fame, too. Until a few

years ago, Honda Gold Wings were assembled in Marysville, OH which helps to explain why Ohio ranks third in the nation in motorcycle registrations.

The famed Mid-Ohio Sports Car Course is just a couple of hours' ride north. In mid-summer, it hosts AMA Vintage Days. That event includes the nation's largest motorcycle swap meet as well as AHRMA vintage road racing, motocross, flat track and trials competitions.

Day 331:
Las Vegas, NV
San Bernardino, California used to be the unofficial "home town" of American motorcycling but new rules restricting off road riding on private property, an increasingly restrictive business environment, and sky-high real estate prices are all contributing to an exodus across the state line into Nevada. Dynojet, a company that dominates aftermarket performance tuning, has already made the move.

Las Vegas Motor Speedway may be the closest major track to any American city center. A busy CCS club racing scene uses the "old" track outside the speedway oval. The facilities out there are primitive but the layout is more challenging than the infield course at the NASCAR track, so amateur racers prefer it.

Harley riders can take in the Laughlin River Run – the largest meet of its kind in the Southwest. Off road riders benefit from an abundance of public land.

Day 332:
Portland, OR
With a great track (Portland International Raceway) right in town, it's not surprising that Portland is home to a thriving club racing scene. The Oregon Motorcycle Road Racing Association has a great rivalry with their Washington state counterparts just up the road in Seattle. Between those two clubs, local riders can get on track dozens of times a year. But the Portland scene's not all about knee-dragging. It's a "ride 'em, don't hide 'em" kind of town where guys (and a disproportionate number of gals) ride cool old Triumphs, Guzzis and Vespas as daily commuters. The northwest has miles of logging roads that are great for dual-sport riding, too.

Day 333:
Concord, NH
The capital city of New Hampshire is just 20 minutes from New Hampshire International Speedway. NHIS is home to Penguin Racing School, one of the country's oldest and most respected riding schools, and to the Loudon Road Racing Series – their monthly events draw over 300 amateur racers from as far south as New York and Washington.

Laconia Bike Week is by far the biggest cruiser and custom gathering in the northeast. Last but not least, riders of dual-sport and adventure bikes can spend a lifetime exploring the forests that stretch north to the Canadian border.

Day 334:
Montreal, Canada
Every American motorcyclist who's gone to Europe has seen the abundance of bikes on the streets and noticed the friendly acceptance of motorcyclists by non-riders. They all come home thinking, "Why can't America be more like that?"

There's one place in North America that *is* like Europe – the Canadian province of Quebec. All summer long, Montreal throngs with motorcycles. Local racers practice at Mt. Tremblant in the nearby Laurentian mountains – it's one of the continent's prettiest tracks. There's an excellent motocross track right on the edge of town, too.

Those things *might* explain why most of Canada's motorcycle racers seem to hail from "La Belle Province" – take ex-AMA Superbike star Miguel Duhamel or his dad, 1970s racing legend Yvon, for example. But its more likely the result of Quebec's uniquely, um, aggressive traffic. After riding there for a while you'll realize that posted speed limits and even red lights are really just suggestions.

As you might imagine, the region offers no end of great dual-sport riding (especially in the fall when the maple trees change color.) Even Canada's best *English*-language motorcycle magazine, Cycle Canada, recently moved its office from Toronto to Montreal.

Of course, there is the Canadian winter to contend with. But Montreal's also home to the world's biggest *snowmobile* manufacturer.

Most Beautiful

Like human pulchritude, motorcycle beauty in the eye of the beholder. So if your personal favorite is not on this list, feel free to scratch off any one of these and write in your own candidate. Your opinion is as good as mine! Still, for the record, here is my top ten, with the proviso that I've limited myself to production motorcycles – customs and full-factory racers were not considered, although you'll note the presence of a few production racers.

Day 335:
MV Agusta F4 (1998-present)
This jewel was originally built around a four-cylinder 750cc motor and is now available as a 1000. The motor was conceived by Ferrari and the chassis was designed by Massimo Tamburini with the resources of the Cagiva Research Center in Varese, Italy. Tamburini (the "ta" in Bimota, incidentally) has created a number of beautiful bikes including the Ducati 916 but this is his masterpiece. Who cares if it's not as fast as a Suzuki GSX-R available at 1/3 the price? It looks twice as fast on the sidestand.

Day 336:
Harley-Davidson XR750 (1969-present*)
This bike replaced the aging KR as Milwaukee's production racer, used mainly in AMA flat track

competition. The bike was designed by Dick O'Brien, who ran Harley's racing department, and Pieter Zylstra but it's safe to say that no one actually "styled" it. The XR is a perfect example of form following function – unencumbered even by brakes in the first few years of production! (*The first XR750s were sold as complete motorcycles but as more and more riders and teams chose to build race bikes on custom frames, H-D began selling mostly motors only. The company still sells a few motors each year, though they are shipped disassembled.)

Day 337:
Ducati Supermono (1993)
Pierre Terreblanche had a tough act to follow when he replaced Massimo Tamburini as head of the design department at Ducati. The Ducatisti were scathing in their criticism of Terreblanche's 999, when it finally supplanted the iconic "916" series. Nothing can change the fact, however, that the South African designed the most beautiful Ducati of all: the tiny, perfect Supermono production racer. The chassis and cycle parts are still impressive, the motor is an elegant adaptation of the 916 twin and it's all wrapped in a skin reminiscent of some shark or ray.

Day 338:
Honda CR250 Elsinore (1973-82)
Soichiro Honda hated two-stroke motors and for the longest time he refused to let his company build two-stroke racers even though it put them at a huge disadvantage. In the early '70s it finally became apparent that it was impossible to make a four-stroke

motor light enough and powerful enough to be competitive in the burgeoning 250cc motocross class. When Honda finally caved in, his firm made the CR250 Elsinore. The early Elsinore with twin shocks and aluminum tank and fenders remains the quintessential "dirt bike."

Day 339:
Triumph Speed Twin (1937)
The 500cc vertical twin motor was conceived by Val Page but the overall design of this bike was the responsibility of Edward Turner, who ruled Triumph as a (somewhat) benevolent dictator. This motorcycle set the basic "look" of British motorcycles for the next 30 years – the heyday of the British industry.

Day 340:
BMW R69S (1960-'69)
This is still *the* classic BMW, especially the early models with Earles forks and plunger rear suspension. Nowadays, we tend to think of these bikes as reliable transport for the tweed-jacket set but in the early '60s, a tuned R69S made for a very effective endurance racer.

Day 341:
Honda CR110 (1962)
A motorcycle, like a poem, is not finished when there's nothing left to add – it's finished when there's nothing left to take away. Nothing proves that better than Honda's 50cc production racer. Even though Honda's factory team used 50cc twins, the production model's single was exquisite, with gear-driven double

overhead cams and a dry clutch, all wrapped in cycle parts that could almost have come from a 10-speed racing bicycle. A bare 8.5 horsepower pushed stock CR110s to a top speed of 90 miles an hour – Making this poetry in (surprisingly fast) motion.

Day 342:
Suzuki Katana (1981-'84)
This unique-looking bike is usually described as "Star Wars-inspired." It was created by an outside consultant, Target Design, from Germany. The design team was led by Hans Muth, who was also instrumental in the creation of the BMW R90S motorcycle and BMW 2002 car. Interestingly, Target initially showed a very similar design for an MV Agusta motorcycle in 1979 but that machine never saw production.

Day 343:
Vespa (1946-present)
Piaggio was an aircraft manufacturer until the end of WWII when the company was forced to reinvent itself, just as Italy was in need of cheap, practical transportation. Enrico Piaggio himself designed the first Piaggio scooter but the end result was homely. It was nicknamed "Paperino," the name given to Donald Duck in Italy.

Piaggio asked Corradino D'Ascanio, an aeronautical engineer, to redesign the scooter and when D'Ascanio unveiled his prototype, Piaggio said, "It looks like a wasp!" The name Vespa – Italian for "wasp" – stuck.

Day 344:
DKW RT 125 W (1939-'50s)
This simple, piston-port two-stroke was designed just before World War II by Herman Weber. After the war, German patents were seized by the Allies by way of reparation. The popular DKW was copied by BSA (which marketed it as the Bantam) and Harley-Davidson (trademark: Hummer.) If imitation is really the sincerest form of flattery, this must be the most flattered motorbike ever made. Deservedly so, since despite the fact it was sold as cheap transportation, the original design was very elegant.

Lessons, Track Schools and why you need them

Every beginning motorcyclist should start with the excellent RiderCourse new rider school offered by the Motorcycle Safety Foundation but your training shouldn't end when you get your license. Improved motorcycle control skills can make the difference between life and death on the road. Just as important, it's a lot more satisfying to ride well than it is to ride poorly.

Thanks to extraordinary brakes, suspension and tires, modern motorcycles can be ridden out of trouble, allowing you to avoid almost any accident. But no rider will use all her bike's capabilities in that moment of stress unless she's already learned those capabilities.

That said, the streets are no place to push the limits of your bike or yourself. That's why the next step in rider training is usually either taken off-road or on a race track – even if you never plan to actually race.

The following list of schools and training courses is not exhaustive (although some of the courses are exhausting!) They're not arranged from best to worst – rather they are listed according to the degree of "raciness" in the curriculum. These are all established programs with great reputations but there are other excellent schools across the country. A more comprehensive listing can be found in most issues of the authoritative Roadracing World magazine.

Day 345:
Motorcycle Safety Foundation
The RiderCourse program is available in virtually every American city and you don't even need a motorcycle to take it. In most states, an MSF certificate exempts beginners from the practical portion of the motorcycle license test. (www.msf-usa.org 800-446 9227)

Day 346:
Trials Training Center
Ironically, you can learn a lot about riding fast on smooth roads by learning how to ride very slowly over the roughest possible terrain. The best place to try motorcycle trials riding – a sport in which competitors attempt to ride over around and through a variety of natural and man-made obstacles – is at the Trials Training Center in Tennesscc.

The TTC tailors programs to students' needs, can supply all the equipment needed and best of all, provides meals and accommodation in a gorgeous setting that could easily double as a millionaire's hunting lodge. It has enough varied terrain to get beginners off on the right wheel or hold a round of the world championships. All in all, the TTC offers a great, safe setting in which to improve basic skills. Should you really take to trials riding, you can also (obviously) get much more advanced training here as evidenced by the way Geoff Aaron a multi-time U.S. champ comes here to work out. (www.trialstrainingcenter.com 423-942 8688)

If you live on the West Coast, Tennessee is a long way to go. Motoventures offers a similar program (without the deluxe lodge accommodation) near Temecula, in between San Diego and Los Angeles. (www.motoventures.com 951-767 0991)

Day 347:
C.L.A.S.S.
Reg Pridmore won the first-ever AMA Superbike championship. Now he runs this school at tracks across the country. The name stands for Controlled Learning of Advanced Street Skills, which tells you that while the setting is a race track, the focus is on practical machine-control. The typical student is mature and many regulars return over and over, treating the school as a track day. Many of these repeat customers bring their own bikes but the school can provide everything you need.
(www.classrides.com 805-933 9936)

Day 348:
Kevin Schwantz School
The charismatic Schwantz is another ex-world champ who's opened a school. The program is similar to Spencer's, although the tracks couldn't be more different. Schwantz's school is based at Road Atlanta, which is a fast, flowing natural circuit that is harder to learn but far more rewarding than the Vegas layout. The school's principal is a naturally outgoing and amusing storyteller even if you do get the sense he's said it all before. Most students use school-provided Suzuki GSX-R600s. (www.schwantzschool.com 800-849 7223)

Day 349:
Penguin Roadracing School
This has been half of Jerry Wood's family business for decades (he's also America's pre-eminent motorcycle auctioneer.) Penguin usually operates at New Hampshire International Speedway, making it the closest track school to Boston and New York. Classes typically include a mix of student and school bikes. (www.penguinracing.com 978-297 1800)

Day 350:
California Superbike School
Keith Code has run this school, usually on one of the several track layouts at Willow Springs on the outskirts of Los Angeles, since motorcycle wheels were chiseled out of stone.
(www.superbikeschool.com 323-224 2734)

Day 351:
Motocross schools by guys named Gary
The MSF offers beginner-level one-day dirt bike schools in most parts of the U.S., which are a good starting point. The two most-established motocross schools in the U.S. are run by Gary Bailey (based in Virginia) and Gary Semics (based in Ohio.) Both schools are focused on riders who have already reached an amateur/competitive skill & confidence level. (Semics: www.gsmxs.com 330-424 9295, Bailey: www.garybailey.com)

Day 352:
American Supercamp
The harder you ride, the more likely it is that you'll
find yourself sliding your motorcycle. For great
riders, this doesn't mean the loss of control, it's
merely the point where things get interesting. Danny
Walker's school uses flat track racing techniques on
tiny dirt bikes. Don't let those "kid's" bikes fool you:
this is serious stuff. No school will ever make you
faster for less money. Great value and highly
recommended. (www.americansupercamp.com
970-223 0525)

Day 353: Preflight Checks

Before every flight, pilots walk around their planes, visually inspecting them to ensure airworthiness. Once in the cockpit, they continue this elaborate preflight ritual with a carefully memorized and itemized series of instrument and control checks.

It's no less important to ensure that your motorcycle is roadworthy. The Motorcycle Safety Foundation (www.msf-usa.org) has an excellent 63-point checklist they call T-CLOCS (for Tires, Controls, Lights, Oil & fuel, Chassis, and Stands) that you can download and print out. Although few riders are so exhaustive before every ride, it's a great weekly habit and a must after taking your bike out of winter storage, or the first time you climb on a new-to-you machine. Art Friedman, the ex-editor of Motorcycle Cruiser magazine once pointed out that if you ride daily, the best time to do a pre-ride check is at the end of your ride, so you'll have time to fix any problems before the next ride begins.

Here are ten essential things to check before you set off.

1. **Look it over!**
It's a statement of the blindingly obvious, but *look* at your bike. Not just the side you approached from, either. Walk around it, and look at it from a low angle. Is anything leaking? Cracked? Loose? Keep your bike clean enough that small changes are noticeable. There are lots of nuts and bolts on a motorcycle. If you only want to look at a few, examine brake caliper pinch

bolts to ensure they are tight. Check the pin or bolt holding the front brake lever to handlebar.

2. Tires
Check that you've got two of 'em. Just kidding. Always check your air pressure – preferably with the same gauge. You'll find normal loss rates of up to 2 psi per week, so in a month tires can get dangerously low. Examine the tread area for damage.

3. Chain and sprockets
Make sure your chain is lubricated and that it has the appropriate amount of slack. If your chain has a master link, look at it! If your chain breaks, your motor's countershaft sprocket can jam it against the engine cases with enough force to break them – and write off your bike. If your bike has a shaft drive, look for weeping or leaks and listen for abnormal noises from the rear hub.

4. Brakes
Roll the bike and stop it with the front brake and back brake. Hydraulic brakes – particularly front brakes – should feel firm, not spongy. The brake lever should not move far enough to get close to the handlebar. Any change in brake feel should be investigated.

5. Throttle closure
Twist the throttle and release it. It should snap shut.

6. Fluid levels
Check oil level and color. Confirm fuel level by looking in fuel tank (if the tank is visually accessible)

or at least by checking the fuel gauge. Make sure tank petcock(s) are in the "on" not "reserve" position. Check coolant level (this can usually be done by looking at the overflow container. Don't open the radiator if the motor is hot!

7. Lights/horn/mirrors
Check the function of all lights, especially brake lights and turn signals. While you're at it, check the position of the mirrors. Honk the horn. Don't really lean on it if you're getting a pre-dawn start, unless the next thing you want to check is the bullet resistance of your leathers (not typically very good.)

8. Paperwork
Make sure you have your driver's license and proof of insurance with you. Know the renewal dates for your vehicle license and insurance.

9. Helmet visor/ear plugs
Make sure your helmet visor is clean. Use earplugs. Think: Will you ride into the evening? If so, make sure you have a clear visor to install for the trip home.

10. Mobile phone
Bring one, especially if you're riding alone. Before you ride off into the sunset, make sure that you have a way of summoning help if you ride off over an embankment. Even if you have a phone, you should still file a "flight plan." Always make sure someone knows where you're going and when you can be expected to arrive.

Day 354: Buying a used motorcycle

There are lots of ways to buy a used motorcycle. You can shop at big-city dealers and look at expertly reconditioned bikes being sold with the remainder of the manufacturer's warranty. That's an expensive but relatively low-risk option. At the other extreme, you can search for a motorcycle on the Internet and buy it sight unseen. You might find a bargain or rarity that way, and it might even be delivered one day, and it might even be as advertised. In between those two extremes, there are local newspapers and web sites, auctions and swap meets, and tiny hand-written notices on laundromat bulletin boards.

Obviously, unless you're dealing with someone you know is trustworthy (or have a friend who can examine a bike for you) you should only buy a bike that you can go and look at. Never inspect a bike in the dark. If possible, you should always bring a friend with you – ideally an expert mechanic, but even a complete amateur is another pair of eyes. Unless you're looking for something very specific, if you decide you want it, it's still usually a good idea to go to the nearest Starbucks for a cooling-off period.

Obviously, to be sure you're getting a peach and not a lemon, you need to check more than ten things, but the list that follows covers ten key areas. For more information, check out Motorcycle Owner's Manual by Hugo Wilson, or The Complete Idiot's Guide To Motorcycles by Motorcyclist Magazine, Darwin Holmstrom, and Jay Leno.

1.)   **Know who you're dealing with**

Any reputable seller will have a title (unless you're buying an antique.) Make sure the VIN number on the document matches the one on the bike. Don't be afraid to ask for the seller's driver's license as well. If the names on the license and title don't match, or the address on the license doesn't match the address where you're viewing the bike, ask why not. If the answer isn't plausible – and preferably, verifiable – walk away. If the seller seems offended that you asked, run.

Ask how long the seller's had the bike and why he's selling it now. There are reputable "flippers," who are either good amateur mechanics or pros moonlighting out of their garages, but they are few and far between. If you know you're dealing with one of those people, fine. In general, however, if it's not really the seller's personal bike being sold for a valid reason, you should avoid it.

2.)   **"Never raced"**

The truth is that an expertly maintained race bike will be in better shape than many street bikes. If you are shopping for a track-day bike, attend a few of your local club races. Walk around and see which racer's pits are clean and well organized. Take note of the local hotshots who keep it rubber side down. At the end of the season, you'll see a bunch of For Sale signs in the pits and buying a bike this way will always be much cheaper than converting a street bike for track use.

That said, unless you're going to do methodical research, an ex-race bike is best avoided, especially if the owner is *lying* by selling it as "never raced." Look for small holes drilled in brake caliper bolts or in the sump plug. (The holes are used for lock-wire, which is mandatory for racing.) Avoid bikes with tires that have blobs of melted rubber hanging off the edges, and never ride on the street with tires marked 'racing' of 'off-highway use'.

3.   **"Never crashed"**

Bikes fall over. A tip-over in the driveway results in harmless cosmetic damage but a hard crash can leave invisible handling problems even after all the bodywork and broken stuff has been replaced. Here's how to know the difference: Almost all factory bodywork is plastic. Most aftermarket bodywork is fiberglass. If you can see what looks like a woven pattern on the back of the bodywork, the original plastic was crashed off. If the bike really fell over in the driveway, the damage will be random gouges and chips. A bike that's gone sliding down the road has parallel scratches. Be suspect of aftermarket clutch covers or other parts at common points of contact.

Even if there's no evidence of a bike having been raced or crashed, look it over carefully to see if it seems straight. Beware of bikes with frames, engine cases or other metalwork that have been extensively polished.

4.   **Has the owner warmed it up?**

If the owner knew you were coming, walk directly to the bike and feel the motor. If the owner has warmed it up, you should be suspicious.

5.   Will he let you take if for a test ride?

If you've come with a friend (read: hostage) the owner has no reason not to let you take a test ride. If you've come alone and he says he's afraid his bike will be stolen, offer to take him along as a passenger, or follow you in/on whatever vehicle you used to get there. Don't buy a bike you can't ride.

6.   Before riding, do a full preflight check

If the owner claims to use the bike regularly, it should be in good running condition. If she doesn't keep up with basic maintenance, who knows what serious problems might be lurking? If for any reason it fails a thorough preflight check you should probably keep looking.

7.   Look at the condition of the "consumables"

Tires, brake pads, chains and sprockets all wear out. Just because they're worn, doesn't mean the bike's a bad buy. If they need to be replaced, however, you should deduct the cost of those parts from the price you're willing to pay.

8.   Be realistic about options and accessories

Although a few factory options like anti-lock brakes or hard luggage add value to used bikes, you should ignore the claimed value of aftermarket accessories. No modern motorcycle needs a loud exhaust or expensive race-quality shock absorber. As for the often-seen offer of "helmet included" – ignore it. The shock-absorbing foam in crash helmets deteriorates with age and even a helmet that looks perfect can be useless in a crash.

9.   If you find the bike you want, search the title

There are a number of title-search companies, such as www.abika.com, but your first step should be to call the state's DMV or your local police department and check the VIN (by this point, you've already confirmed that the number on the title matches the one on the bike.) Note that in California, the state requires vehicles to be continuously registered – if the bike you're looking at has been off the road for a few years, you could find yourself facing hundreds of dollars in lapsed registration fees.

10.   Put aside enough money for top-quality protective gear

Your first year on a motorcycle is, by far, the most dangerous year. Make sure you start out with a good helmet, jacket, gloves and boots at a minimum. Don't blow your whole budget on a motorcycle and make do with a garage sale helmet, ski gloves, and high-top sneakers.

Day 355: Track hacks and training aids

If you're committed to riding as well as you possibly can, you'll soon need a training bike. The best way to train depends on the kind of person you are and the kind of riding you do. Nowadays, it seems every top racer has a tiny play-bike rigged up specifically for "sliding" practice. While you may never intend to skid your motorcycle on purpose, don't discount the merits of doing some of this short-track-style training; it's fun, safe, and the skills you develop can save your life when you find yourself caught in heavy rain or – heaven forbid – when you come across a diesel spill on some highway cloverleaf.

If you're a hard-core sport rider or would-be racer, you'll want a track-day bike – something fast, reliable and repairable that you can thrash once a month at your local race-track.

On the other hand, if you're more inclined to tour or cruise, you'll benefit from a reliable trail bike that you can take to the nearest off-road area and jump, bounce and slide around on. That kind of informal off-road riding is a great way to tune up your balance, reflexes and confidence without putting yourself under any pressure. Even if you don't have access to a full-scale trail riding area near your home, there's probably some vacant lot where you can train on a trials bike, since they're ridden at walking speed.

Finally – and I hate to break this to you – virtually every great motorcyclist is also a bicyclist. For pure fitness, road riding (think Lance Armstrong) is best, while mountain biking is a great way to develop balance and control along with strength.

The following list is not a ranking. It gives you a couple of good play-bike suggestions, two excellent choices for used track "hacks" and one interesting new bike that comes track-ready. For off-road use I've suggested two great trail bikes and a trials bike. Last but not least, I've offered one good value in a basic road bicycle and a comparable mountain bike.

So… go drag a knee; slide the rear tire; land a jump; pick a perfect line through the rocks. And yes, get into shape to do it. You'll find your motorcycle riding is more fun, more controlled, and safer as a consequence.

1. **New play-bike: Honda CRF150F**
Small enough and light enough for teenagers or the average female rider, but spunky enough for a 180-pound guy to use for a day of easy trail riding. An adjustable rear shock makes this one bike the whole family can ride (not at once!) The electric start is another user-friendly trait. Manufacturer's suggested retail price: $3,640. (www.powersports.honda.com)

2. **Used play-bike: Honda XR100**
Honda made this venerable little bike for decades with practically no changes. Over the years, many motorcycle racers have taught themselves to control a sliding motorcycle by purposely sliding an XR on a tiny dirt oval. What they learned at 15 miles an hour, they applied at 150 miles an hour. Despite their diminutive size, these Hondas withstand endless abuse. Their only downfall is that racers snap them up

for training, keeping used prices high. Expect to pay about a thousand bucks for an XR that is in good shape and few years old.

3.   **Used track-day bike: Suzuki GSX-R600**
If you want a bike that you can truck or trailer to a track day, your best bet is to buy a three to five year-old race bike that someone else has already set up for track use. Buy something common – that way spare parts, setup advice and mechanical help will be easy to find. There are more 600cc "gixxers" on the track than any other bike.

Cosmetics are not important but finding a straight one is. If you're in doubt, ask the seller if you can take the bike to your local Computrack shop for a measurement. Prices will vary depending on condition and equipment, but you should find something sound for $2,000 to $4,000. Prowl the pits at your local race-track on the last race weekend of the season, when local hotshots are broke!

4.   **Used track-day bike: Honda CBR600F4**
You don't need a truck or trailer to go to a track day. All you need is a bike that you can ride to the track. A CBR is comfortable enough to ride 100 miles to the track if you have to – and more important, comfortable enough to ride back after an exhausting day of knee dragging. It's also affordable, especially the pre-'01 models that had carbs instead of fuel injection. You should be able to buy a mechanically sound CBR600F4 for $2,500 to $3,500. Again, cosmetics aren't an issue, so buy an ugly one and spend the money you save on tires!

7. Street-legal trail bike: Suzuki DR-Z400S or Honda CRF250L

Suzuki's respected dual-sport bike is a surprisingly good trail bike, in spite of its 290-pound weight. You can easily ride to the trails, even if you live in the middle of a big city and the nearest trails are an hour or two away. This mid-sized thumper dominates its category for a good reason, though it's not cheap at $6,200. Honda's new CRF250L is getting rave reviews, is cheaper at $4,500, and is probably an even better choice for riders under 200 pounds.

8. Used trials bike

Trials riding, in which motorcycles are ridden over and around obstacles at slow speed, is a great way to improve your skills with minimal risk. Although they may look spindly and fragile, the bikes are actually very rugged. Montesa, Gas Gas, and Sherco are among the popular makes and the best way for you to choose one is to track down the nearest trials club and see what bikes are popular in your region. It's a specialized sport, so don't give up if you ask at a local motorcycle dealership and are met with a blank stare.

A five year-old 250 is all you need to putt around in the nearest vacant lot or even to compete as a novice. You should be able to find one for $2,500. Begin your research at the Trials Training Center website, www.trialstrainingcenter.com.

9. Road bicycle

Before you spend thousands of dollars on carbon-fiber bodywork and a titanium exhaust to reduce your motorcycle's weight by 10 or 20 pounds, look in the mirror: you should probably lose that weight yourself. It's not a coincidence that almost all motorcycle racers train several hours a week on bicycles – improved cardio fitness allows them to concentrate better and stay relaxed when riding hard and being light and lean allows them to accelerate harder and brake later. Want to beat your buddies in the Stoplight Grand Prix or the Local-Twisty-Road Championship? Hit the road, Jack, with two wheels but without a motor.

REI co-op stores (www.rei.com) are found in major cities across the U.S.. REI's own brand of bicycles is Novara. The "Divano" road bicycle combines reasonable component quality with comfortable ergonomics for less than $700.

10.   Mountain bicycle

Riding a bicycle off road is a great way to improve your fitness and tune up your balance and reflexes. REI's Novara line includes the "Torero," a solid entry-level mountain bike with front suspension. You should find this for under $500. Remember this, however – it is as important to wear a proper helmet on your bicycle as it is on your motorcycle!

Day 356: Must-have Gear and Accessories

Being a motorcycle rider means never having to
answer, "I don't know" to the question, "What do you
want for Christmas?"

If the person asking you is on the Forbes 400
list, your first answer should always be "A BMW
R1200GS," but if your friends are not quite so well-
heeled here are ten bits of kit you'll be guaranteed to
enjoy for many years to come. Each is best-in-class
and each offers great value.

1.   **Aerostich Roadcrafter one piece riding suit**
Absolutely, positively the best all-purpose riding suit
on the market. You might think it makes you look like
a motorcycle nerd the first time you put it on but once
you've experienced its practicality and protection
you'll never want to ride in anything else. Two
gigantic zippers make getting into it or out of it a
breeze. Speaking of breezes, the Roadcrafter provides
terrific ventilation, allowing you to ride fully
protected in weather from near-arctic cold to tropical
heat. Made from indestructible nylon with even more
indestructible ballistic patches in areas that might,
some day, make contact with the road. Lots of soft
armor too so God forbid you should crash but if you
do, do it in this suit. At $$897, it's expensive but oh,
so worth it. (www.aerostich.com)

2.   **Shark crash helmets**
For years, helmet manufacturers strove to conform to
"Snell" helmet standards. The Snell standard reflected

the needs of race *car* drivers, not motorcycle riders. In fact, the big Japanese companies that dominate the American market sold harder helmets in the U.S. than they did in Japan or Europe, specifically so their helmets could withstand the Snell test – a test that requires the helmet to survive *two* impacts in the same spot.

The problem is that those harder helmets are more likely to transmit a shock to the wearer's brain. The result is that while they are vastly better than nothing at all, they are not as good as a "softer" helmet. Shark is a French company that makes crash helmets with "crumple zones," reducing the risk of concussion. Top of the line Sharks sell for $400-plus, but all Shark designs have the same shock absorption technology. (www.kneedraggers.com)

3.   **Power Commander**

Modern fuel injected motorcycles are set up to run very lean – a result of manufacturers struggling to pass environmental regulations. Most bikes run a lot better with a slightly richer fuel-air ratio at low rpm and partial throttle openings. To make that change, you need a programmable engine control unit, like the ones sold by Power Commander. Typical sport bike applications sell for about $400. Although installation is straightforward, it's even better to program your bike on a dynamometer, which is a job for a pro.

4.   **Gaerne Altus waterproof boots**

Lots of riders have a rain suit but few have waterproof boots. These fine Italian boots by Gaerne (pronounced "gar-nay") combine race-quality protection with a breathable waterproof liner. They are completely waterproof and comfortable enough to wear even if it's not raining. The manufacturer's suggested price is about $225, though Internet shoppers will find them for about 25 bucks less. (www.gaerne.com)

5.   **Dainese Wave back protector**

Virtually all racing organizations now require riders to have a back protector, as well as the usual helmet and one-piece leather suit. But a back protector isn't just for racing. You should wear one whenever you ride. Dainese's three-layer "Wave" is the product of this Italian firm's relentless dedication to research that helps to make us all safer. The Wave has an expanded metal mesh impact absorber that's light and breathable. Once you put it on, you won't feel it, but you will feel a little more confident. About $190. (www.dainese.com)

6.   **Cruz Tools**

Most motorcycles come from the factory with a "tool kit" that leaves a lot to be desired. Cruz Tools make custom tool kits for Harley-Davidsons and for metric bikes. The tools are high quality and well chosen. Each comes packaged in a folding nylon pouch. The company also makes a great tool pack that off-road riders can wear around their waist. Cruz' top-line kits sell for from about $80 to $170. (www.cruztools.com)

7.   **Galfer braided steel brake lines**

Many motorcycles are sold with rubber brake lines. They work fine when new but as they age, rubber lines soften. The result is a spongy brake feel that can hide other problems. Galfer, a Spanish company, makes stainless steel brake line kits for most sport bikes and many other models, too. Front brake kits for motorcycles with dual discs are usually about $85. Installation is easy enough for any shade tree mechanic. (www.galfer.com)

8.   Aerostich courier bag

Aerostich founder Andy Goldfine also started America's national Ride To Work day (www.ridetowork.org). If you're going to ride to work, though, you need a way to carry your lunch, laptop and the Jenkins file you brought home to read before realizing that yesterday was "Two Wheel Tuesday" on SpeedTV and you'd spend the evening glued to the television. That's where this courier bag comes in. It's big enough to hold a day's necessities and made to last a lifetime. Best of all, an ingenious design allows you to sling it over one shoulder with ease and have it stay in place behind you while you ride. Cost: $87. (www.aerostich.com)

9.   Tire gauge

If you're at a loss for a stocking stuffer, every motorcycle rider needs at least one tool – an accurate tire gauge. It can be as simple as the straight, pen-shaped type that will fit in a sleeve pocket or a "pro" dial gauge. A Cruz Tools dial gauge is about $17.

10.   Spider Grips

Another great stocking stuffer is a new set of grips. You might think these are just simple pieces of molded rubber but you'd be wrong. Spider Grips are made from two different densities of a high-tech polymer that work together to dampen vibration while providing lots of grip friction. The result is less fatigue on long rides and reduced "arm pump" if you're riding at race pace. In colors to match most bikes. About $17. (www.spidergrips.com)

Day 357: Going into hibernation

If you live in the northern states or Canada, you will inevitably stop riding for a few months each winter. Even if you're lucky enough to live in the sunbelt, you might need to put a bike into storage for a few months for any number of reasons. If you take these simple steps, when you get back to your bike it will be as good as you left it. But consider yourself warned: if you don't prepare your bike for prolonged storage, you may come back to an expensive repair.

If at all possible, you should store your motorcycle indoors. A heated garage is ideal, but a location that gets cold and stays cold is better than one where your motorcycle will repeatedly freeze and thaw. If you have to store it outside, get a specialized cover that will keep rain and snow off it, but will allow water vapor to pass through, so that it doesn't trap condensation.

1.   Protect your gas tank and fuel

Fill the gas tank with fresh gas and a fuel stabilizer, like Sta-Bil. Filling the tank as full as possible reduces the risk of rust forming inside steel tanks. Adding fuel stabilizer prevents the gas from oxidizing over the winter. Come spring, although you can just burn off stabilized fuel, it's better to drain it (or pump it) out of your motorcycle tank and burn it in your car, where the stabilizer is diluted in a larger quantity of gasoline.

2. Drain the carbs

If your bike has carburetors, you need to drain them. Turn off the fuel petcock(s). Many carbs have a drain plug in the bottom of the float bowl. Loosen that plug and drain out the gas. If your carbs don't have drains, you can either remove the bowls and empty them, or at least run the engine until it burns off the fuel in the bowls and stalls. If your bike has fuel injection, this advice does not apply.

3. Tend your battery

Most motorcycle batteries will not survive a winter's neglect. Buy a specialized trickle charger, like a Battery Tender, and attach it to your battery. Unless your garage is going to get very cold, you can leave the battery wired into your bike. If there's a risk of your battery freezing, put it on the charger indoors.

4. Check your anti-freeze

If your garage or shed will drop below freezing, make sure that your anti-freeze is fresh and mixed to the proper ratio. Remember that all race bikes and many track-day bikes have water only in their cooling systems! They should be drained or, better still refilled with anti-freeze for the winter.

5. Wash and wax

Wash your bike thoroughly. Grit and grime will trap water, and spattered bugs can be corrosive. Make sure it's nice and dry. Wax all the painted parts, but don't buff them down until spring. Exposed metal parts can be coated with specialized sprays like S100 Corrosion Protectant, or you can use WD-40 or even chain wax.

Come spring, those coatings should be washed off before your first ride. Loosely plug your exhaust with a rag or bunched up plastic bag. That will reduce condensation inside it, and discourage squirrels from filling it with nuts.

6.   Change the oil

Some people feel that over the winter, oil will absorb water. According to this theory, it should be changed in the spring. The problem is that old oil has acids in it that can corrode your motor over the winter. The best advice is to change the oil prior to cold storage. Remember that your motorcycle might have a separate transmission and or drive shaft that also runs in oil. Change it all.

In the old days, pros told riders to pull the spark plugs from their bikes, squirt a bit of oil in each cylinder and turn the motor over a few times to coat the cylinder walls with oil. That's still a good thing to do if you're leaving your bike more than a few months. However, on some modern bikes pulling the plugs is a real hassle. Marinas sell a product called fogging oil that can be sprayed into the air intake while the engine is running.

7.   Check your brake fluid

Hydraulic fluid traps water that can cause corrosion in brake master cylinders and calipers. High-temperature "racing" brake fluids are especially prone to absorbing water. If your brake fluid looks at all suspect (if it is darker than honey, for example) you should drain, refill, and bleed your brakes.

8.   Are your tires tired?

Tires do simply age, whether you wear down the tread or not. If your tires are nearly due for replacement, now's a good time to pull your wheels off. Over the winter, take them to your dealer for new rubber.

If you want to get another season out of them, don't store your motorcycle near a source of ozone – like the compressor motor in a freezer, or other electric motors that run all the time. Some people like to store their bikes with both tires off the ground "to prevent flat spots." That's never a problem with modern tires but it *is* good to prevent tires from freezing against cold concrete floors. The popular opinion is that tires should be fully inflated or even over-inflated (no more than 120% of the maximum pressure listed on the sidewall!)

9.   Miscellaneous lubrication

There are many points on a motorcycle that require periodic lubrication. Throttle, clutch, and brake cables; chain; steering head, swingarm, and wheel bearings, etc. To get a list of them, and to find out what lubricant is recommended for each application, you will need to check a Clymer or Haynes manual for your specific motorcycle.

10. Cover it up like a Republican congressman caught with a trannie hooker

If you're storing your motorcycle in a heated garage, all you need is an old sheet to keep the dust off it. If the garage is unheated, buy a motorcycle cover that will not trap condensation. Resist the temptation to go out in the dead of winter and start it up, just to hear it run; that will do more harm than good. When spring rolls around, make sure to perform a thorough pre-ride inspection before taking it out.

Day 358:
Worst movie not on "Worst Movie" list: Brown Bunny

When this film premiered at the Cannes Film Festival, it was so savaged by the critics in the audience that the writer/director/star Vincent Gallo stood up on the stage and promised then and there never to produce another movie. The story follows a motorcycle club racer on a journey across the U.S.

Besides its general awfulness, Brown Bunny is best remembered for the explicit oral sex scene with indy film heroine Chloe Sevigny that Gallo wrote into the film. Hey, if you're going to blow your film career...

Day 359:
Best product not on "Best bits of kit" list: Dumonde Tech chain lube

Dumonde Tech's Rod Faulkner is a guru of high tech specialty lubricants. His bicycle chain lubes free up lost horsepower on motorcycles, too. It's not that easy to find, but it's worth looking for.

Day 360:
Most beautiful motorcycle not on "Most Beautiful" list: Britten V-1000

Britten was perhaps the most creative stoner ever to come out of New Zealand. His death from cancer in 1995 deprived the world of its best motorcycle designer at the time.

Day 361:

Best race not on "Epic Races" list: The Pike's Peak Hillclimb

One of America's great races, in one of America's most scenic regions. Usually held early in July. Worth the trip to Colorado, and when you're not watching the race you'll be surrounded by thousands of miles of great roads (and fire-roads, for the dual-sport crowd.)

Day 362:

Best rider not on any of the "Best Rider" lists: James "Bubba" Stewart

Stewart, whose signature 'Bubba Scrub' move has changed the sport of MX and SX, has never quite lived up to the expectations he set when he utterly dominated the 125cc class. If he'd crashed less, he would almost certainly have established himself as the most naturally talented motocross racer of all time.

Day 363:

Most amazing motorcycle not featured anywhere else in this book: Dan Gurney's Alligator

The iconoclastic Dan Gurney, who was successful both racing cars and building race cars, is also a serious bike nut. His 'recumbent' style Alligator motorcycle is a rare example of a modern bike designed from a completely clean sheet of paper.

Day 364:
The best motorcycle blog that you have never heard of (that isn't www.bikewriter.com)
Hands down, it's www.bikesandbuddies.com, put up by a guy named Kevin Moore. Tell him I sent you.

Day 365 -- Last but not least, something that's not trivial at all: Staying alive

Riding a motorcycle safely on the street means doing three things. First, you must cover the basics: you must know the rules of the road; ensure that your motorcycle is safe to ride; know how to operate it, and wear a helmet, gloves, boots and jacket at a minimum. That comes from good basic training like the RiderCourse offered by the Motorcycle Safety Foundation.

Second, riding on the street is an exercise in information processing. Doing it safely means taking in a lot of information and filtering it to determine which drivers need extra attention and what situations need to be avoided before they present an imminent risk. The rate at which you can process that information is the most important factor in determining a safe speed.

Third, when all else fails, safety hinges on having the motorcycle control skills you need to safely stop before you hit trouble, or to enable you to steer around trouble. If you pay attention to all three of those areas almost all motorcycle accidents are avoidable.

This list is not a list of "the ten things you need to do to be safe." There are far more than 10 important safety tips. For more information on this subject, read any or all of these excellent books:

- The Motorcycle Safety Foundation's Guide to MOTORCYCLING EXCELLENCE
- Proficient Motorcycling: The Ultimate Guide To Riding Well, by David Hough
- Total Control: High Performance Street Riding Techniques, by Lee Parks

With those provisos, here are ten tips to make you a safer rider...

1. **Watch drivers, not cars**

Look inside cars to make sure drivers are driving, not talking on cell phones, doing their makeup, making out, shaving (don't laugh, I've seen it!) or eating a gooey hamburger with two hands while steering with a knee. If you see any of those things, create extra space.

While many drivers will change lanes without signaling or shoulder-checking, they will still telegraph moves like that with body language. If you see a driver ahead of you turn his head to glance into your lane, expect him to move into it whether he signals or not.

2. **Make eye contact**

If you can't see a driver's eyes, he can't see you. Always be aware that you're in a driver's blind spot. How can you tell? Look for his eyes in his mirrors. If you can't see his eyes, move to a safer position.

If you see another driver shoulder check, but don't clearly make eye contact, assume he has not seen you. If you see a car waiting to enter a road you're on, or turn left in front of you, and the driver looks in your direction but does not definitely meet your gaze, assume she hasn't seen you.

3.) Look out for vehicles with obvious danger signs

Pay particular attention to vehicles with crash damage – they are usually owned by accident-prone drivers. Cars that have missing or malfunctioning turn signals and brake lights, or are obviously un-roadworthy should also be given extra room. Even a really filthy car is a sign that its owner doesn't like driving. People who don't like to drive are not good at it.

4. Play "What if?..."

When you're out riding, ask yourself what you'd do if the ladder on that painter's van a hundred yards ahead of you blew off and landed in your lane. Or, what you'd do if that car waiting to enter the road pulled out right in front of you. Decide what evasive action you could take and mentally practice it. *When it is safe to do so* (on empty roads) you can even practice real evasive maneuvers or hard stops.

5. Understand target fixation

When something dangerous happens in front of you, it's human nature to fixate on that threat. That's a deadly mistake. After you identify a threat, pick your escape route. Look where you want to go.

It's too late to teach yourself about target fixation when you're in a real panic situation. Learn to see escape options, not threats, by playing 'what if?' Pick a line, focus on it, and *make your motorcycle go there* in informal practice sessions while riding.

6.   **Make your small size an advantage**

Motorcycles are vulnerable because they are small but that size can be turned into an advantage. Never just float along in the middle of your lane in traffic. Instead, position yourself in your lane so that you can see around vehicles in front of you.

If you're like most American motorcyclists, you drive ten times as many miles as you ride. As a result, in a panic situation, you may tend to act as if you're in a car, not on your bike. For example, if traffic comes to an unexpected halt on a multi-lane highway, you should aim for the gap between lanes for extra stopping space. Your car can't fit through there, but your bike easily can.

7.   **Know your brakes**

If you only – or even mainly! – use your rear brake, you need to stop riding on the street right now and go get more advanced training. In a panic stop, all motorcycles derive the vast majority of their stopping power from the front brake.

Learn to trust your front brake, even if it's raining or you need to slow down in mid corner. Practice applying your brakes and adjusting your cornering line in the middle of turns. You never need to grab a big handful of brakes on a modern motorcycle – two fingers will usually suffice.

Get in the habit of riding with your index finger on the front brake lever at all times; you don't need your whole right hand to twist the throttle.

8.   Never "run wide"

The most common type of single-vehicle motorcycle accident happens when a rider feels that he has entered a turn too fast and chooses to run off the outside of the bend. *Never, ever* do this! In the vast majority of such crashes, the rider could have made the bend with ease; he merely lacked the confidence to do so.

On any modern sport bike, the limit of cornering adhesion is well past the point where your knee is touching the pavement. Even on cruisers and touring bikes, you can lean past the point where things are starting to drag.

If you find yourself entering a corner too fast, *do not look at the edge of the road.* Gently apply the brakes to scrub off as much speed as possible. Look towards a safe exit line. Countersteer and lean off the inside of your bike. Lean the bike as far as you need to.

In a worst-case scenario, it is almost always safer to suffer a low-side crash because you leaned too far than it is to ride off the road on your wheels and crash in the ditch.

9.   Never just go on green

If you're waiting at a red light, don't take off like Ricky Gadson the instant it turns green. American drivers all seem to think that yellow lights mean "floor it." With that as the prevailing attitude, many drivers are effectively timing the red light, expecting to clear the intersection before cars can enter it on a fresh green light.

Motorcycles can easily accelerate much faster than cars, but car drivers don't realize that. They may well be thinking, "I can get through before the traffic starting off can cross my path." If you prove them wrong, the fact that you had the right of way will be a small consolation indeed. In general, assume that car drivers have underestimated your speed, because they often have.

10.   **Don't go away mad**
Although riding helps a lot of us to keep our sanity, don't storm out of the house after a fight with your spouse and get on your motorcycle to clear your head. Riding while angry or distracted is as dangerous as riding drunk or stoned. Your goal is a state of relaxed awareness. Don't ride to find that mental state; find it, then ride.

(If you're wondering why the only day's entry that contains absolutely essential knowledge appears on the last page, instead of the first page, it's because I know most motorcycle riders are impatient types who will probably flip straight to the back of the book to see how it ends! — MG)

About the Author

Mark Gardiner has been a motorcyclist over 40 years. He's the author of the cult-classic memoir *Riding Man* (which is currently in development as a feature film at Escape Artists/State Street Productions.) He was also the subject of the acclaimed documentary film *One Man's Island*.

In addition to *Riding Man*, he's the author of *Classic Motorcycles*, and *BMW Racing Motorcycles: The mastery of speed* (with Laurel Allen.)

Mark writes a monthly column in the UK magazine Classic Bike, and posts a monthly column called 'Backmarker' on the MotorcycleUSA.com web site. He's the author of the popular and often-controversial blog at Bikewriter.com.

Away from the world of motorcycles, Mark is known as an expert on the subject of cultural branding. He's the author of *Build a Brand Like Trader Joe's*. He also wrote the autobiographical novel *Year of the Raven*.

He lives in Kansas City where he is a partner in the the ad agency re: (www.revolutionaryoldidea.com)

Made in the USA
Middletown, DE
18 December 2018